P9-AFE-644

B $16.75

How to Live Aboard a Boat

How to
Live Aboard a Boat

Janet Groene

HEARST MARINE BOOKS

New York

**HEARST
BOOKS**

Copyright © 1983 by The Hearst Corporation.
Manufactured in the United States of America.
All rights reserved.
No part of this book may be reproduced or used
in any form or by any means—graphic, electronic,
or mechanical, including photocopying, recording,
taping, or information storage and retrieval systems
—without written permission of the publishers.

Library of Congress Cataloging in Publication Data

Groene, Janet.
  How to live aboard a boat.

  Bibliography: p.
  1. Boat living. I. Title.
GV777.7.G76 1982   797.1′2   82-11971
ISBN 0-87851-217-9

Hearst Marine Books
224 West 57 Street, New York, N.Y. 10019

DEDICATION

To all those ashore and afloat who helped
Gordon and me along the way: a writing job
here, the offer of a dock there, a bucket of
ice, an understanding or forgiving word, the
loan of a car, the use of a washer and dryer,
dinner invitations that included hot showers,
letters from neglected friends, the sharing of
bountiful catches, and wise advice tactfully
given.

Contents

Preface

~~~~~~

S o you want to live aboard a boat? Come on in, the water's fine. It isn't the purpose of this book to tell you whether you need a ketch or a yawl, how to anchor, or how to take a sunsight with a sextant. A sailboat was home for ten years for my husband Gordon and me, but your home could be a houseboat, powerboat, trawler, even a trailerable boat. We chose to head for the Southeast, the Keys, and the Bahamas. Your dream could be to lose yourself in the South Seas, live on a mountain lake, probe all the waterways of the Tennessee Valley or California Delta, or to drift forever in the rivers and canals of Europe.

Our choice was to cruise constantly, but in short hops and never in passages of more than three or four days. You, however, might choose to sail around the world nonstop, or to live on board at a local marina, going to the office every day.

For some, living aboard means a retirement life, or a way to give the children unforgettable memories of travel. We had enough savings to last a couple of years and then we planned to get whatever jobs we could find. Then, as we began selling our books and magazine articles, we earned all the money we needed as we cruised. Perhaps you have savings, a steady income, or plan to make a living as you go.

We were in our thirties when we started out. You may be younger, wanting to have an adventure before settling down. Or you could be ready to retire. We are a husband-wife team. You could be a couple, a foursome, a family, college chums, or a loner.

Living aboard, as this book will point out, is not one way of life but a different *modus vivendi* for each person or group who chooses to make a hull a home. Yet we all have many things in common: our love for boats and the water, too little room, too much mildew, never enough money or time for harvesting all the wonders of an Earth that is covered more by seas than by lands.

For everyone who wants to live on a boat of any size or type, here's how.

9

Living on the water brings many rewards.

PART ONE

THE GREAT GETAWAY

Chapter 1

Don't Break Your Rice Bowl

~~~~~~

W e rocketed back into the welcome shelter of Port Everglades on a rising tide and a friendly following wind. It had been an exhilarating, exhausting day of sunburn, rope burn, and bridge burning as we faced our first day aboard our 29-foot sloop *Sans Souci*.

Everything we owned had come south in our Volkswagen bus. The boat, purchased a few months earlier, had been in storage while we went back to shed the job, our home, and most of our possessions in Illinois.

We had never sailed in our lives except for a one-hour sailboard rental during a business trip to Freeport. Yet, thanks to Gordon's experience as a pilot, we were never mystified by sailing, pilotage, navigation, mechanical problems, or anchoring techniques.

For the first three nights in Fort Lauderdale we stayed in a hotel, dreading the cost because we no longer had an income. Then we moved aboard to spend two weeks commissioning the boat. Today had been our first sail and tomorrow we would start a cruise down the Florida Keys. But suddenly, tonight, we had nowhere to go!

There had been other thudding culture shocks in our transition from comfortable suburbanites to routeless, rootless liveaboards. One occurred when we could not cash even a cashier's check on the day we arrived in Fort Lauderdale. Another was the refusal of our travelers check in a discount store where we had bought galley equipment. Now, with nowhere to anchor, we motored into a seedy marina and paid a dockage fee that, computed on a monthly basis, was more than our mortgage payments had been on a ten-room house back in Illinois.

13

We slept fitfully, wondering what new defeats we would suffer in our victory over the rat race.

The best way to describe the liveaboard life is probably to list what it is not. It is not a way to escape yourself, a bad marriage, taxes, or responsibility. It is not an island idyll, a free lunch, a free ride, or the way to write The Great American Novel. Nor is it the solution to your addiction to pills, tobacco, or alcohol. These days, with more people living aboard than ever before, it is not an escape from crime, pollution, and crowding. Nor is it, since the lifestyle has become more commonplace, a way to gain envy, awe, approval, or even a mild gee-whiz. Half the time it isn't even comfortable, let alone chic.

Yet living aboard your boat can be a low-cost, mobile way of life. It can be more exciting, educational, rewarding, and inspiring than anything you've ever done. It can be a warm, family-bonding approach to raising children. It is a way to travel without a suitcase, with time to live among a variety of cultures. You may test yourself to your physical, emotional, spiritual, and psychological limits. It is a way to grow, to achieve, and to take control of your life.

The first step toward boat living comes well before buying the boat. It is a step of commitment, of honest agreement with yourself and your partners that this is something you truly want to try. A boat can be a shrewd investment, but not if you buy on impulse and sell in a panic after a family showdown. Any raw edges in your relationship will unravel quickly in the close quarters of boat living, so hammer it all out on shore where you'll still have room to throw crockery at each other.

There are two international organizations for liveaboards. Homaflote, P.O. Box 4192,N. Fort Myers, FL 33903 is open to everyone who lives aboard or wants to. The Seven Seas Cruising Association, P.O. Box 38, Placida, FL 33946, offers membership to sailors who have no other home, who have lived aboard for at least a year, and who are recommended by two other members. Both organizations put out invaluable monthly newsletters, and even those who do not qualify for membership in S.S.C.A. can subscribe to the bulletin.

Even though you've now come to a decision in the privacy of your boudoir, it may be best not to make a public announcement just yet. It took us three years to get our ship together. If we had been yammering about it all that time we would have bored our landside friends beyond all caring. Keeping mum was better socially, and better at work. We didn't appear to be as desperate as we really were when selling out, and, most important of all, it gave us the option of backing out without looking like fools.

Everyone who lives aboard has a different story of how it all got started. For many, moving aboard comes at a pivotal time of life such as graduation, marriage, divorce, retirement, or getting the children through some milestone such as potty training, college, or marriage. For a lucky few, the decision to move aboard comes through some windfall. While cruising the Bahamas we met one young man who had made a million-dollar commercial sale in real estate. He arranged to take his $100,000 commission over a period of ten years, and set sail. For others, one straw breaks the camel's back and they leave the job or spouse in a cloud of haste and hatred.

Most of us, though, simply got the liveaboard bug and began building towards our goal slowly and steadily, over months and even years. Gordon had spent years to gain his goal in corporate aviation. Now he had a job he enjoyed with just the kind of company he always wanted to fly for. Both of us liked living in a small city like Danville, our neighbors were our best friends in town, and the corporate future seemed star-spangled.

Then word came that a valued friend had died, in his early 40's, of a heart attack. Another friend lingered with cancer, and a third told us he had an incurable disease. Social Security taxes went up. Real estate taxes ballooned with inflation. The crime rate was getting worse. We weren't getting any younger. We began to look more closely at what we wanted, and whether we really needed all the money that was sieving through our checkbook. We decided that we wanted to be together all day every day, to cruise, and to pay the piper tomorrow—if tomorrow ever came.

"You wouldn't have any choice if you had children," many people have grumbled to us. Yet, after moving aboard, we met many people who lived aboard *because* of their children not in spite of them. Some parents felt that they wanted to get their kids out of the drug scene. Others simply wanted to share such an experience with their families.

In any case, hammer it all out ahead of time. We've seen too many marriages come unglued because one partner wanted to stop cruising and start cradling. Even with older couples, a common problem is that one wants to live ashore close to the grandchildren while the other wants to continue combing the beach. If you really want to move aboard, the children can adapt even easier than you can. If you really don't want to live aboard, admit it and stop blaming anybody else.

Will you really be able to hack liveaboard life? The answer may surprise even you. The sea has a way of cutting one down to size, especially when it becomes your home. Seasickness can be a problem. Although Gordon had blithely weathered a typhoon while crossing the Pacific, aboard a troop ship, he is always miserable for the first few days out of port. And I, a lifelong camper and practiced boat cook, spent one Thanksgiving in tears because the pumpkin pie slopped out of the pan, despite gimbals, and messed half the galley.

One couple spent three years, working every weekend and after work, to build their own boat. They lasted only a few months because they found out they (1) hated boats, (2) hated boating, and (3) hated each other. Another couple labored for years to build their dream boat before the Missus' first sail. On their first day out in sheltered water on a calm day, she went absolutely bonkers with fear. We've known three people who never could overcome their fear of sailing *after* they moved aboard! Even iron-gutted weekend sailors find that living aboard is something else again.

The way to rehearse living aboard is so obvious, we're amazed that so few people try it. Bareboating sounds like a costly vacation, especially when you are scraping and saving to buy a boat of your own, but it is cheap compared to the financial and emotional Dunkirk of going through the entire move-aboard scene and then finding you despise the water, the boat, the lifestyle, or all of the above.

Most of the bareboaters we met while cruising have filled every bunk aboard, in order to split costs. It's often more fun this way, but it is not a preview of what life will be like when you have everything you own aboard, must do all the boat chores yourself, and must operate on a year-round budget rather than a vacation spree.

For a week, most of us can put up with almost anything. Then we fly home and flip the sandy, salty laundry into the automatic washer and dryer. That's why you need two, three, or four weeks aboard the type of boat you want to live on, *with* the person(s) you plan to live with.

Cost is about $3,000 for two weeks on a 44-foot sailboat; a little less for a 36-foot trawler. If you plan to live on something smaller, try a 32-foot boat for $1,000 a week or less. Houseboats are available in a wide range of sizes, prices, and locations. For a list of houseboat rental firms, send a stamped, self-addressed, business-size envelope and $2 to Botebooks, Box 248, DeLeon Springs, FL 32028. Power and sailboat charters are found in the national boating magazines.

By the end of your third week aboard a bareboat you will have encountered many things a one-week charterer does not have to worry about: laundry, changing the bunks, cleaning, provisioning, getting mail, a wide range of weather conditions, some mechanical problems, nightly anchoring or docking problems, getting about on shore without a car, the boredom of rainy days, and living with limited facilities and space. Bareboating is a rehearsal that can save months of work, expense, grief, and, later, failure.

If there is one axiom we'd beg you to remember during your move from house to boat, it is "Don't break your rice bowl." Sure, there were some people in Danville we should have liked to tell off before we split. Still, you never know when you might need a job recommendation, a reference from an old boss, a job lead from an old colleague, or a personal reference from a former neighbor.

A gradual, friendly, cooperative transition not only buys you goodwill for the future, it allows you time to do things prudently and economically. It has always been a juggling act to sell one home and buy another without having to make double mortgage payments for a month or two. It is even trickier to quit your job, sell the house and furniture, and move into a boat—especially a boat that is hundreds of miles away—and have it all come out even.

Should you take the final steps such as quitting your job and selling your home? If so, when? If you can get a leave of absence, do so by all means. No matter how boring, Mickey Mouse, or ill-paid this job may seem now, it could look like a sinecure after your first all-standing jibe, your first sniff of dry rot, or your first night in a wet bed. Whenever possible, leave doors ajar.

Selling the house is another matter, especially in these inflationary, uncertain times. If you sell out now, the same money may not buy you so much as a garden shed in ten years. But, if you rent the house, you could come back to find the tenants and termites have teamed up to win the real estate demolition derby.

Since we had no family ties in Danville it was easier for us to sell out. We'll never know if we would have made more money by keeping the house. We do know that we no longer had to worry about mortgage payments, pest control, paying someone to manage the rentals, the cost of upkeep and repairs, meeting the insurance, and the ever-present dangers of fire or vandalism or a lawsuit from someone who slipped on the front steps. Besides, the equity in the house represented the bulk of our savings, and we needed the money for cruising.

Most liveaboards who rent out their homes have excellent luck, but others had to leave the boat on the hook somewhere while they flew home to straighten out real estate horror stories—tenants who skipped town owing months of rent, tenants who ran out on big fuel bills, or tenants who left the house filthy or who stole fixtures.

Hanging on to the furniture is even more a problem than keeping the house. Furniture seldom appreciates as a home does. Storage space is costly in both monthly rental and in deterioration. One friend of ours found that all her heirloom linen had turned to powder while in a storage locker. To keep things from rusting, rotting, and mildewing, you'll pay a premium price for a warehouse where temperature and humidity are controlled. "Free" storage can be even worse if Uncle Harry decides to turn his basement into a rec room, or the Petersons, who have your safabed in their attic, are transferred to Anchorage.

All the beloved bits and brickabrack that clutter our lives ashore are anchors clinging to the would-be liveaboard. Choosing the boat and selling the house are easy compared to parting with your Tom Lehrer records, or your Dresden collection, or the home movies you took while you were stationed in Germany.

This was a very difficult time for us, made tougher by the stock characters we all encounter in certain of life's dramas. You've seen families torn apart by quibbling over the belongings of a relative who died. Many of these same conflicts occur when you break up housekeeping. We were lucky to have supportive families and loyal friends, but we've known liveaboards who carried scars for years from these fracases.

The other stock characters in this skit are the people you must deal with when selling out: antique dealers, skinflint used-furniture dealers, long-lost relatives who want back every gift they ever gave you, auctioneers, and the general public. Steel yourself for a lot of shoving from all directions, and keep your balance. The best is yet to come.

Chapter 2

Choosing Your Liveaboard Boat

∞∞∞∞∞∞∞∞∞∞∞∞∞∞∞∞∞∞∞∞∞∞∞∞∞∞∞∞∞∞∞∞∞∞∞∞

W e promised that this would be a book for everyone who wants to live on a boat, not a book about how to choose a sail rig or what kind of ground tackle you'll need for anchoring off Nassau. Choosing a boat is like choosing a spouse: you're committing your ego, safety, happiness, and a good chunk of cash. When the boat will also by your home the decision is even more of a burden—financially, socially, and practically. Not only is it a huge step, but it's also an expensive and time-consuming one if you have to study, correspond, and travel to look at boats.

The purpose of this chapter is to make suggestions about choosing your boat for its *liveaboard* merits, whether you're thinking of a houseboat, trawler, trailerable, sailboat, or powerboat.

Because we lived in a small, landlocked city where there were no boats, we drove to Fort Lauderdale, where we found a veritable supermarket of boats for sale. Annapolis, Newport, and San Diego are happy hunting grounds for sailboats. So is Holland, Michigan. For houseboats, you might travel to Nashville, Chattanooga, or Sacramento. Fort Lauderdale is also full of powerboats and trawlers. Our favorite source for used boats has always been the classified section of *Soundings*, a monthly boating newspaper, available at most marine hardware stores. (For subscription information, write to them in Essex, CT 06426.)

If you're shopping for a new boat, go to the biggest boat show you can find. The schedules are printed monthly in most of the national and regional boating publications, in a calendar section.

For a look at European boats you might try the London or Paris boat

Boat shows, like the International Boat Show in Miami Beach, are a good place to start scouting the market.

shows, held in January, or the Southampton show held in late summer. The Netherlands, Greece, Norway, and Ireland have shows in March. There is an in-the-water show in September at Gothenburg, Sweden.

The Miami International Boat Show is the world's largest show and one of the very best. Annapolis, Maryland, has huge powerboat and sailboat shows in the water in the fall. The mammoth New York Boat Show is held indoors in January. There are in-the-water shows held in Fort Lauderdale in November and in St. Petersburg in early December. On the west coast, big in-the-water shows are held at Newport Beach and Marina del Rey. The California Delta Boat Show is held in Alameda, the heart of houseboat country, at the end of April. Every major North American city has a boat show; some, such as Seattle and Miami, have two or more shows a year.

Look, look, look. The more you know about boats and boating, the more shopping shortcuts you can make. Read boating magazines, go to boat shows, talk to boat owners. Get out on the water as much as you can to learn the language of boating. By being on and around boats, and listening a lot, you'll soon learn which boats have a good reputation, and where to look for each boat's weak points.

By listening to boat owners complain you'll learn that Brand X is known for a wood core that rots under the fiberglass, that they can't keep an exhaust system in Brand Y, or that Brand Z's rigging won't last more than five years. If you can find a boatyard that specializes in a particular brand of boat, nose around to see what their most common problems are.

If you're looking at a boat that operates in fleet service, you have a research goldmine. Talk to the maintenance chief or fleet owner about what works and what fails. A houseboat fleet operator once told us that the plywood floors in every one of his Spongebottom Houseboats rotted out in two years. A bareboat fleet manager in the Virgin Islands said every hatch in his fleet of Bedwetter 41's leaked from the day the boats were delivered.

Even if you decide to go ahead and buy a Spongebottom Houseboat or a Bedwetter 41, you can use this sort of information as a bargaining point. Some good bargains have been made by those who know that a production motorsailer that was popular a few years ago develops dry rot under the cap rails, or that Paperthin Boats were using shoddy fiberglass lay-up in their 1978-79 hulls.

Like everyone else, we started out searching for a diesel auxiliary sailboat. We found *Sans Souci* and liked everything about her except her gasoline inboard engine, a brand which we'd been told had crankshafts made out of popsicle sticks. Mentioning this, we made a low offer and got the boat. Gordon has spent all his professional life flying gasoline-powered airplanes, and knows something about living with volatile fuels, so we knew we could operate the boat safely. When we checked out the stories of the bad crankshafts, most turned out to be instances of operator neglect. We got a good boat and a good bargain, and had ten years of smooth, flawless performance from a "pariah" engine.

Lets's talk about some of the general types of boats which make good homes. Even if you've been a committed rag sailor or sportfisher for years, read on. The boat you like for boating, and the boat that will make the best *home* for you, are often different—as many liveaboards learn too late. You might be happier, for example, living aboard a houseboat and sailing in a dinghy or boardsailer. Or living on a deep-draft sailboat but having a fast little fizzboat for exploring and fishing the shoals. Or living at the dock in an old-pauper-priced power boat and using your savings to charter once a year in some exotic, faraway port.

Sailboats

In Favor:

There is more grace and beauty in a sailboat than in almost any other manmade thing, and artists through the ages have celebrated this beauty. Wind is free, so your fuel costs can be practically nothing. Sailors are a particularly friendly crowd, independent, resourceful, and clannish so you'll belong instantly to a proud fraternity. The right sailboat-home can take you around the world for peanuts, and mendable sails get you home even if the engine conks out. There is a huge choice of sailboats in every design, boatbuilding material, and size. The motion of a sailboat, properly set up for existing conditions of wind and sea, is an easy, natural delight. In addition to serving as your home, a sailboat can race and so can also be your recreation.

Against:

The wind doesn't always blow, and when it does it is often too much wind, or from the wrong direction, or both. Because sailboats are sleek, you get less actual living space per dollar, per hour of labor if you are building, and per foot of length than in any other type of boat. A sailboat that has no engine is rare, so a lot of room is taken up by the engine and by mountains of sails. Sailboats tend to have deeper draft than other boats of the same length, and this limits your choice of cruising area. The more time you will spend at the docks, the less practical a sailboat will be for you. While sailboats are natural and comfortable under sail, they are less comfortable under power than boats designed to run exclusively under power. While wind is free, sails, fittings, and rigging are not. Finally, we find that most sailors run their engines far more than they'd planned to.

This Cheoy Lee 42 sails to Nova Scotia every summer from New York, and provides a year-round home for her owners.

Motorsailers, Trawlers

In Favor:

You may have the best of both worlds in a seakindly motorboat that is also designed to sail. Most such designs have inside steering stations, so you'll be out of the weather. Socially, you're in a happy no-man's land loved and accepted by both sailors and powerboat folks. There's a large choice here, ranging from motorsailers that really sail, to trawlers with mere steadying sails and powerful engines. Many long-distance, cruising-boat families have trawlers or motorsailers. The good ones are handsome, spacious, and ruggedly seaworthy.

Against:

While you have the best of both worlds, you also have the worst of both worlds. Some motorsailers are poor sailers; some are poor powerboats; some are both. Such boats have more windage, making them harder to control in a breeze than some sailboats. You may lose living space because you're carrying both sail(s) and engine(s).

Powerboats

In Favor:

In a powerboat you have speed, power, and comfort, a boat you can fish from seriously, and extra power for all the luxuries such as refrigeration and full lighting. Older powerboats with gasoline engines are often a spectacular bargain for liveaboards who will spend a lot of time at the dock, because the boats are too expensive to run. Sold cheaply they still have spacious and comfortable—often downright luxurious—accommodations.

Powerboats that are properly designed are not only fast, but are economical, seaworthy, and capable of ambitious cruises. Many of the new diesel motor yachts are miserly on fuel. You get a lot of living space for the overall length and for the dollar, excellent resale value if you choose the boat wisely, and years of dependable motoring. And it's easier to learn to drive a powerboat than to learn to sail.

Against:

Fuel costs may soar again. Your cruising is limited to where you can buy fuel and how much you can afford. Noise, vibration, and exhaust fumes go everywhere with you. Power yachts have a lot of windage, and can be tricky to control. You're totally dependent on mechanical devices. A flashy power yacht may be a more likely target for thieves, highjackers, and corrupt port officials.

Houseboats

In Favor:

In a houseboat you get more livability for the buck than in any other type of boat. They don't pretend to be yachts, although lately there has been a blurring of the distinction. Houseboats are boxy, which means you get more usable space per foot than in any other type

This is a trawler-type, called the Island Gypsy. She would make a good liveaboard boat, although she is too high and has too much glass to be a good sea boat.

Island Gypsy's *main salon is bright and airy for such a small boat.*

Her galley is all you need, including a view. You could steer and cook at the same time if you had to.

On board a 48-foot Seamaster, the mast stands in the middle of the cabin. Chairs and lamps must be secured so they can be stable even in a lot of motion underway.

On board this Poole 95, the salon can become quite sumptuous. Note the maritime necessities, among them, handrails and rounded corners.

Potted plants and a back porch, lots of storage and light. This is Island Gypsy, seen on page 26.

The salon on board Sea Cloud, the largest privately owned yacht in the world. She served for years as the residence of the ambassador to Russia. She is a 353-foot square-rigged ship, requiring a crew of 45 to sail her. She illustrates living aboard in the grandest style.

This is really a home afloat, with TV and cut flowers. Note the rack for fishing rods overhead.

Teak cabinets, carpeting, and champagne for the liveaboard grace this Bertram 54.

of boat. Many houseboats are not made for saltwater boating, and use non-marine materials at a huge cost savings. House and housetrailer materials are used, at mass-production prices. You save on the purchase and on repairs and replacements. Doors, windows, fixtures are all standard home-builder sizes in many houseboats.

There is a great choice of hull type, size, power options, and brands. You can get a houseboat with outboard engine(s), sterndrive(s), or gasoline or diesel inboards of almost any size. You can even have a very large houseboat with a very small kicker, to use on lakes which have restrictive horsepower limits. Draft is shallow, ranging from tiptoe-deep pontoon boats to deep-vee hulls, so most houseboats are ideal for shoal waters. In many freshwater locations throughout the country, you'll see few boats of any other type, because houseboats are simply the best choice for these waters.

Against:

Houseboats are, socially, the country hicks of boating. Even other powerboat owners may turn up their noses at your square, unseaworthy box. Most houseboats have poor directional stability, making them tiring to drive on long trips. They have acres of windage, making them difficult to dock or anchor in any wind. The same non-marine materials that make a houseboat less expensive than a yacht make it less durable than a yacht, especially in a salt water area. Unless you buy a houseboat that is specifically built to use on salt water, you'll face severe rusting and corrosion problems within months after you venture onto the deep.

Another debit for houseboats is that even though they give you more cubic footage than any other design, they often make poor use of this space. You will rarely find a houseboat with more than one head (toilet), even though sail and power yachts that are barely more than thirty feet now have two heads. Layouts are often awkward. For example, in many designs you have to enter the head through one stateroom. Lately the trend has been toward free-standing, house-type furniture, and away from built-ins. This means loss of the big bins and drawers that are found under bunks and settees. You may need to customize your houseboat-home to make it as space-efficient as other vessels.

This 46-foot houseboat, undergoing renovation, has its own workdock and tender.

Jim Wynne's design, the Goldcoast 50 built by Coastal Yachts in Richland, Mo., has three cabins and two or three heads. Note the number of on-deck locations for private rendezvous.

Boatel's budget 50-footer sells for about $50,000, draws 22 inches and sleeps up to 14.

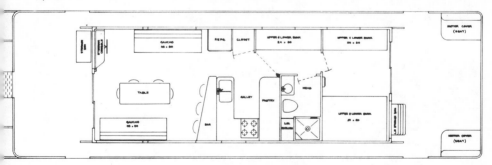

The foredeck of a houseboat is more like a wonderful front porch.

This boatman, a houseboat liveaboard for 7 years, enjoys the sun while his boat remains shaded and cool.

Hunter Yacht's 37-footer has a cutter rig for ease of handling.

The Hunter 54 can be raced to Bermuda, but also has private staterooms each with its own companionway. She stows the dinghy in a sort of garage in the transom.

Trailerables

In Favor:

Until recent years, liveaboards-to-be might not have considered a trailerable boat because most were too small to live aboard. Today there is a large choice of liveable sailboats, powerboats, and houseboats which can be towed with a large car or a truck. You have access to every fresh and salt water destination, even landlocked lakes. Instead of having to make long passages to reach, say, Florida from California, you do it by road—at 55 mph. We knew one couple who cruised the Bahamas each winter, and Georgian Bay or the Apostle Islands in Lake Superior each summer. Instead of slogging for weeks up the Intracoastal Waterway, or taking the raw spring and fall winds in the ocean, they made the north-south trips in three or four pleasant days of driving. Although the towing vehicle is an added expense, it also serves as your ground transport, sightseeing bus, extra closet, and, if it has modest camping equipment, weekend camper.

Against:

There is a size limit, of course, to what can be towed on the road so you may not be able to have as large a boat as you'd like. The towing vehicle has to be purchased, stored when you're afloat, maintained, and insured. So does the trailer. Concrete cruising isn't free because you'll pay big fuel bills and turnpike tolls. Tires and other expendables have to be budgeted for. And few people would say that hauling a big tow of any sort is easy or fun.

When shopping for a weekend boat, it's hot news that the boat will get up on a plane in ten seconds, or has a fish-finder thrown in free, or bunks for an entire Cub Scout troop. But you'll be spending most of your time aboard this boat sleeping, preparing meals, and otherwise performing the plain tasks of living. You may not run the engine more than once a week. But you'll go to bed every night, and make breakfast every morning. Any boat is a compromise, but remember that your needs as a liveaboard will be different from those of other boat buyers. The choice of boats today is better, more tempting, and more confusing than ever before. Go into the marketplace with your eyes, your options, and your mind open.

Chapter **3**

Narrowing the Choice

⌘⌘

O nce you've decided what type of boat you want to live aboard, there is still a labyrinth of decisions ahead. Every boat buyer is concerned about price, quality, suitability for his or her own needs, safety, economy of operation, resale value, and other factors. But you'll be *living* aboard, and your choice has to go one step beyond all these.

No matter whether your choice has been big boat or small, old or new, houseboat or sail, every liveaboard has certain biological needs to be met day by day. These require the right bed, the best galley, and a head you can live with.

The Bed

We humans spend a third of our lives in bed. While you might make do with a pipe berth, a quarter berth, or a converted sofa for a week or a weekend, the liveaboard boat's bed is one of her most important—perhaps the most important—accommodations. This bed is for sleeping, romancing, reading, staying in bed with a cold, perhaps even for weathering more serious illnesses. The year of the Hong Kong flu, Gordon and I were both floored for three solid weeks. If you'll be making overnight passages, you also need a berth you can stay in despite rough seas or angle of heel.

Although we've met many liveaboards who managed happily with convertibles, it really is best to have a bed that stays a bed. It's tempting to use the forepeak for storage, and sleep in the main saloon, but it's

One third of your life is in bed. Be sure you'll be comfortable.

Guest quarters on board Sea Cloud.

A special telltale compass is mounted here upside down over the bed. This is not a traditional "sea-berth" but it is on a boat that has crossed the ocean many times: Sea Cloud.

On a 48-foot sailboat, the aftercabin can have windows in the transom, and lots of stowage. Private head is just to the right.

Yes, this is on a boat, a Poole 95, although it's not everyone's idea of live-aboard life.

wearying to have to make up a dinette bunk night after night, year in and year out.

If one of you is sick and wants to stay in the sack for a day, if one wants an after-lunch nap, or if one of you is a lark and others are owls, you need places both for the one in bed and for those family members who want to stay up. Separate "bedrooms" become even more important when there is more than just one person, or one couple, aboard. Children need their privacy too, in a safe place which will be their own for nights, naps, playing, and homework. More later about living aboard with kids.

You may feel foolish at the boat show or showroom, but measure bunk length—either with a measuring tape or by stretching out in it. Some are only six feet long; some are even less. Try sitting up in the bunk to see if there is enough headroom for night-time reading, and/or basic amorous adventures. If you want a double bed that is at least as wide as a standard-size double, measure that too—even if you have to ask the salesman or broker to assemble it. Otherwise you may be fooled because the bunk *looks* large enough compared to the boat's other mini-facilities.

If you're really counting on having a cozy, snuggly double, try that out, too. Some vee berth fillers were designed by the Marquis de Sade; some by Bozo the Clown. The cushions that look so crisp and natty with their pleats or buttons or cording may feel, when deployed, like a bed of broken bassoons. If they are vinyl they'll be cold and crackly in winter and hotter than an oven in summer.

Although it's important to get a bed that is long, wide, and thick enough, beware of getting one that is too big. Those huge, playpen-size mattresses often seen in big aft cabins are very difficult to make up and they require costly custom bedding. We once lived for a week aboard an aft cabin boat with a vinyl-covered mattress the size of Rhode Island. Trying to tuck in the sheets was like trying to give an elephant a massage, and the sheets spat out from under the slippery plastic the first time one us turned over. The other problem with such big bunks is that you may not be able to wedge yourself in in rough seas.

Over the years we've had excellent service from a series of synthetic foam mattresses. Visit a good foam outlet, or a mattress factory, to learn about the various grades of this foam. Some are denser, some softer, than others. You need foam at least four inches thick, five if you can manage it. If you get a thicker mattress it may be difficult to handle, which is a consideration because the mattress should be turned weekly. There may be times when you have to haul it out on deck for drying or airing, and you'll be constantly shifting the mattress to get at stowage areas under the bunk.

Foam rubber, which does have a more luxurious feel, is not good for boats. It holds water, smells rubbery, and weighs a ton. We once spent a couple of weeks aboard a boat which had a double-bed-size foam-rubber mattress that was royally soft. But getting into the under-bed stowage compartment was a job for four marines.

Conventional bedding is best for the liveaboard boat. Sleeping bags can be practical for weekend boats, but they're hot for tropical cruising, difficult to wash, and not very romantic. Crisp, clean sheets and pillow cases atop a fabric-upholstered mattress or cushion are what you have at home and are most homey aboard.

At first, I slaved over a hot sewing machine for hours, customizing and mitering the sheets for our vee berth. Then I discovered I could form an absolutely secure pocket for the foot of the mattress just by taking the two bottom corners of the sheet and tying a knot. After that I bought only flat sheets and never bothered about customizing them. While synthetic fibers don't have the insulating talents of wool or down, I prefer them for boat blankets. Natural fibers smell bad when wet, dry slowly, and are tricky to wash.

One discovery which we're still using after ten years is an electric mattress pad from Patented Products Corporation, P.O. Box A, Danville, OH 43014. Single and double sizes are available in 12-volt or combination 12/115-volt models. If you have full-time household power, there's a large choice of 115-volt sizes and dual control models. The single-bed-size 12-volt pad takes 60 watts, the double takes 80 watts. Even if you use it for nothing more than heating and drying a cold, damp bed before you crawl into it, the electric mattress pad is a gem for living aboard in cold weather. Electricity makes dry heat. Those non-electric, reflective "heating" mattress pads, by contrast, simply bounce back your own body heat and moisture, so they are less desirable for boats.

The Galley

I put the galley after the bed because everybody needs sleep but not everyone likes to cook. One circumnavigator lived for years on almond butter, stoned wheat crackers, and sprouts. That filled his esthetic and nutritional needs and he simply didn't want to bother with more. But since all of us eat, and most of us enjoy the process, let's assume you want an adequate galley. Again, the liveaboard's needs are different from those of the part-time boatman.

The family who lives ashore can cook at home, and warm it up on the boat. They can have their company meals and holiday feasts at home, and make do on the boat with simpler fare. They can stay home on the day the oil is changed, or when major maintenance means tearing up the boat. But your culinary show must go on. That's why one of my prime requisites for a galley is one located away from engine-room hatches. (In some small boats the galley *is* the engine room hatch, alas.) Both the cook and the engineer need and deserve full-time access to their workshops.

It's also a good idea to have a galley that is out of the family traffic pattern. A straight-line galley along one side of the saloon puts the cook in the way of fore-and-aft traffic and, if you sail one tack for a long time, the entire galley is either falling down on you or falling away from you.

Workshop is the word to keep in mind as you choose or build a boat-home, because the galley has to be just that—not a cute little kitchen that has been squeezed down to dollhouse size. You need a sink large enough to wash your pots, a faucet high enough to fill the teakettle, a stove wide enough to hold your big skillet, an oven if you can manage one (although we lived happily without), work space including some space that can be used in heavy weather, stowage space including some that will be accessible on all tacks. If you want a freezer and/or refrigerator, they should be suitable to the boat and its power.

While the galley should be out of the way of traffic and of engine-room maintenance, it should be in the area of best possible ventila-

A *liveaboard galley can be just like a kitchen, with hot running water and double sinks.*

This sea-going trawler shows her seriousness of purpose by her navigational instruments visible in the pilot-house, and by the secure location of everything on board.

This 42-foot trawler has a household type refrigerator, with hooks on the doors.

The straight-line galley is ideal for the cook who likes help, not for the loner-cook. Cook in straight-line galley is always in the way of fore-and-aft traffic.

The galley aboard Bolderson's Nymph Errant was offset from the center of the boat so the engine room could be reached without disturbing the cook.

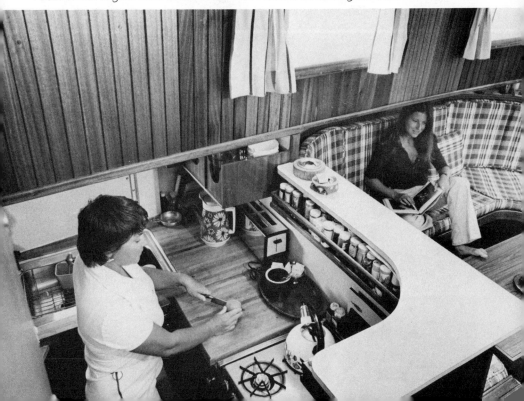

Galley of the Cheoy Lee 42 in dockside mode. Notice the many electric conveniences, as well as the offshore inverted thermos on the left.

Microwave ovens are appearing in more and more galleys.

The dish stowage in this Stamas 44 is well thought out. Note the double sinks near the centerline for best drainage on either tack.

A breakfast counter above the galley is useful for keeping the kids out from underfoot.

Curtains are important, even in the galley, because the view may not always be great, or you may not want to be the view.

On a Blackfin 32-foot trawler, a U-shaped galley is directly opposite a small dinette, which folds down for a spare berth for overnight guests.

tion. Heat, steam, and cooking odors build up in seconds even in large boats, because of limited room and low overheads. One good spot for the galley is, for instance, at the bottom of the ladder that leads below from a wheelhouse or saloon or, on a smaller boat, just below the companionway. Cooking heat can then rise to your boat's "second story" or directly to the outside.

Effective, waterproof vents are essential to good galley ventilation in all winds and weather. Even on fair nights we often had to close up the boat against mosquitoes and sandflies. The more ventilation (but not winds that could blow out the stove flame), the better. You can use a 12-volt automotive fan to help channel away stove heat. Venturi-type vents, installed over the stove, move tons of air and use no electricity. One model is the "Aeolian" from Jay Stuart Haft, 2925 N. Tennyson, Milwaukee, WI 53217; another is the "Vent-o-Mate" from Beckson Marine, P.O. Box 3336, Bridgeport, CT 06605.

Depending on your galley design, you may also be able to add an exhaust fan, kitchen style. Sears Roebuck's Recreational Vehicle Catalogue offers a small (about twenty inches) hood with 12-volt exhaust fan. Beware of two things. In a salt atmosphere, kitchen-type exhaust fans don't hold up well. Also, they have square corners which are a hazard for the cook in rough seas. Shun those recirculating "exhaust" fans which do not expel stove heat but just filter it. We once spent a week in Florida on board a houseboat with such a fan and it was useless for ridding the boat of steamy stove heat. You'll be cooking bacon, frying fish, and sautéing onions aboard. The more fumes you can vent to the outside, the less will congeal on overheads and bulkheads for you to scrub or repaint later.

While other galley equipment will be saved for the next chapter, the table is something to think about as part of choosing the boat. This will be the nerve center, work center, social center—and often the navigation center—of your boat-home. It's one thing on a boating vacation to grab a sandwich in the cockpit. But the table in your liveaboard boat is where you'll have meals including Christmas and Thanksgiving dinners, balance the checkbook, play cards with friends, and do spread-out tasks such as studying charts or kneading a big batch of bread.

If the table is not big enough or versatile enough, and can't easily be made suitable, look for another boat. We've met liveaboards who regretted for years that their motorsailer's only dining table was on the bridge deck and a long walk from the galley. And others whose little saloon had two small tables, but no way for four people—let alone more than that—to sit together.

The equipment you choose for your liveaboard galley depends a great deal on how you want to eat, what energy you'll have available, and what you can afford in both money and space. More about that later.

The Head

The ideal bathroom has acres of room, heated towel racks, a tub the size of a compact car, and maybe a Jacuzzi. We did hear of such a head on a large Feadship motor yacht once, but most of us settle for far less. The Pardey's lived for years with their wooden bucket. Our own liveaboard head was simply a marine toilet, curtained off between the forepeak and the saloon. We managed with marina showers, swimming over the side, a cold-water cockpit shower for after-swim rinses and, at anchor in the dead of winter, with helmet baths and stove-heated water.

One of the greatest hardships of our living aboard was to use marina showers which, in the areas we usually cruised, were often spartan and squalid. Yet we managed because we spent so much time in the Bahamas with its clear, sun-warmed waters. Some marinas have showers so sparkling and inviting, even those liveaboards who have showers aboard use shore facilities. So your need for an on-board shower varies according to what alternatives you have.

In any case, get a separate shower stall if at all possible. We've spent a lot of time aboard boats with showers that wet down the entire head, and it means that you either have to chamois the entire compartment after each shower, or live with the mess until it dries by itself.

Having a shower aboard is not all beer and skittles. Soap scum and mineral scale build up over the weeks, and eventually you have a tough cleaning job. If the shower is fiberglass, you clean it with bathroom cleaners, but getting the build-up out of a teak grating is another

The marble "head" on Sea Cloud *may not match your needs on a houseboat. There is no concession to shipboard motion except the small rail in the shower.*

Perfectly functional, this telephone-shower is hooked to pressure water, and comes with a view outside.

On a 95-foot boat, this shower-tub-towel rack makes perfect sense, although you couldn't call it a head.

A tub with seat, and an angled mirror, make this a complete head on a 48-foot sailboat.

A shower separate from the rest of the head makes both easier to keep clean.

You have to look pretty hard to see the porthole to tell you that this head is on a boat.

matter. Showering aboard means obtaining and pumping more water, heating water somehow, using more energy, more work for the bilge pump, and more moist heat in your boat. One of the nastiest house-keeping jobs of all is cleaning the shower sump. If you add a salt water shower, which is a good way to conserve fresh water, you have the added mess of salt water intruding into your living quarters.

We did make a couple of modifications to our tiny boat that made it easier to live without a shower. Two sink sprayers were plumbed into the pressure water system, one in the cockpit and the other in the head. Even though the cockpit shower was cold water only, it provided us with a thorough fresh-water rinse and shampoo after swimming. The thumb-action trigger was very easy to use, and the spray was satisfying without wasting water. The other sprayer turned the head into a bidet. It was also used to fill a basin with water for washing face and hands. The basin was then dumped into the toilet and the water pumped out.

Little needs to be said about the location of the head(s) except that, when you're living aboard, it's not practical to have an aft cabin boat that has no belowdecks corridor, and a forward head. If you have to go through the cockpit to get to the loo, it's cumbersome at midnight and downright embarrassing to scurry through in your skivvies in the broad light of morning.

One would assume that nothing needs to be said about the head itself, except that we've seen so many grotesque head installations you may need a warning. On one boat, for example, the mainmast sat smack in front of the throne. While it made a good handhold in rough seas, it made mounting the head an athletic event. We've also seen heads so high your feet dangled, and so close to the door there was no room for knees. Close the door and sit down on the head, then decide if it's one you can live with day, night, and Sunday, at sea and in port.

Chapter 4

Equipping Your Boat as a Home

〜〜〜〜〜〜〜〜〜〜〜〜〜〜〜〜〜〜〜〜〜〜〜〜〜〜〜〜〜〜〜〜〜〜〜〜

Just as no one could tell you how to furnish your cottage or condo, no one else knows how you can best make your own hull a home. Remember, this book is not a guide to the equipment you need for boating but for accommodating this boat to *living* aboard.

Most would-be liveaboards have spent thousands of hours and miles and dollars in buying equipment, right down to the last socket wrench and strawberry huller, that they thought could, should, or might be used aboard. Yet until you've lived aboard for a while you don't really know what works, what gets in the way, what's worth having, where money was wasted, and what new items are needed. My recommendation is to move aboard with only the basics, then add new accessories after you're sure of what, and how many, you want.

Some of the things we had in the beginning stayed with us for ten years and were used and appreciated daily. Others took up more space than they were worth; some couldn't stand the sea environment; still others were abandoned reluctantly for lack of room. Many things, of course, are kept on hand for boating emergencies and must be made room for even if they are never used. Other oddments, like Gordon's business suit and notes for a book I never wrote, were kept around just in case they were needed. Only you can decide if you can live without an eyelash curler, a Monopoly game, or a marble bust of Beethoven. Deciding what to take and what to leave behind is a nightmare. Eventually you end up as confused as the man who ran from his burning house carrying only an umbrella and the works of Shakespeare.

Decisions on small things like clothing and kitchenware begin now

55

A welcome mat indicates that this is not a boat just for weekend sailing, but is also a home.

and go on throughout the liveaboard life. Here are some suggestions for liveaboard equipment which should be added before you move aboard or as early in the liveaboard life as possible:

Propulsion

A full discussion of engine choices for your liveaboard boat could occupy an entire book, and does: *The Complete Book of Pleasure Boat Engines,* by Ernest A Zadig (Prentice-Hall). It goes into gasoline engine versus diesel engine, single versus twin, and outboards.

There is, however, one new option that is of special interest to the liveaboard buying a small (under 35 feet) motor yacht: OMC's Sea Drives. While they look like outboards at first glance, Sea Drives are a new concept that places a sealed engine (or two) on the outside of the transom. All the hull space that might have been used for engines is now freed for accommodations, extra fuel or water tankage, or gear stowage.

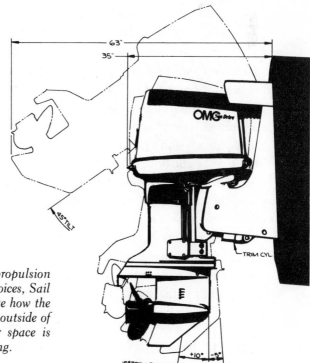

When you're choosing propulsion don't overlook two new choices, Sail Drive and Sea Drive. Note how the Sea Drive attaches to the outside of a high transom. Interior space is freed for stowage and living.

According to OMC, a 33-foot twin inboard boat with a 12-foot beam devotes as much as 190 cubic feet of interior space to engines and related equipment. To replace inboards with outboards means cutting down the transom, with all the related problems. Sea Drive, on the other hand, is designed for use on powerboats up to 35 feet LOA which were originally designed for inboard or sterndrive power.

Before you choose engines for your powerboat, take a look at all the choices—inboard, outboard, sterndrive, and Sea Drive. For your sailboat, look not only at inboards and outboards, but at saildrives.

Lighting

A few years ago, I was looking at a galley design for a new cruising sloop. The galley had everything, and in the right size and the right place to suit me as a cruising cook—except for one thing. I surprised the boatbuilder by pointing out lighting. It was an overhead dome light that at night would turn the fiberglass interior into a dismal cave concocted of shadow and glare. It would be unflattering to people sitting at the table, unsuitable for working or reading at the table, and impossible for a cook who was trying to trim potatoes at the sink or rummage in the reefer for an elusive lemon.

Boats are built, shown, and bought by day. If you shop at night in a brightly lit showroom or boat show, you don't notice that there is too little light, and in the wrong places. Your boat's navigation lighting is required by law according to the type and size of the boat, and the waters, so we won't go into that. (See Chapman's *Piloting, Seamanship, and Small Boat Handling* from Hearst Marine Books.) In addition, you will need a good selection of flashlights, Cyalume chemical emergency light sticks, signal lights, man-overboard lights, and a powerful spotlight.

Liveaboards need good lights for doing all the things one does after dark: preparing meals, writing letters, shaving or using make-up, welcoming guests and reading in bed. You'll find a good choice of lights in all sizes in marine stores. Recreational Vehicle stores and catalogues are also good sources of 12-volt and combination 12-volt/110-volt lights. Through marine stores and catalogues you can also find good, bulkhead-mount kerosene lamps and candlesticks.

The best choice is a total 12-volt lighting system that runs off the accessory battery (it is important to have separate electrical systems—one for starting the engine and another for accessories such as lights, radio, stereo, etc.); 12-volt lights have very low draw and provide good light with little heat, and batteries are easily charged from shore power or by running the engine. If you want a little additional heat, you can't beat the classic Aladdin kerosene lamps for good lighting and a pleasant glow of warmth in the cabin. They're sold in many sizes and materials, in marine stores, catalogues, and hardware stores. There are also 6-volt portable lights in sporty table-lamp styles, sold for camping, but it's costly for the liveaboard to keep buying batteries for them.

You can't have too many lights. After all, you can simply leave them off if you're conserving battery power. Fluorescent lights give bright light for working at the sink, stove, or workbench but are hard on the over-30 complexion. So consider brighter lights in work areas and softer lighting for areas of the boat where you'll be dining or chatting. Over the bunks, cone-shaped shades allow you to focus a bright light on your own book without disturbing a sleeping partner. Bertram powerboats have built-in, automatic lights that go on as you open clothes lockers. If you don't want to be this fancy, mount flashlights around the boat where they can be grabbed easily to look in dark locker corners, the bilge, and the icebox.

In addition to Coast Guard required lights, it's nice to be able to light the deck when you have to do a repair job after dark, are coming home late, or are having guests aboard. On a sailboat, spreader lights fill the bill; on a powerboat look for a high perch where a light or two can be mounted. Small courtesy lights to highlight entries, steps, and other stumbling blocks are a good safety feature and they take very little electricity. If you mount an extra switch over your bunk for these outdoor lights, you can flood the deck with light if you suspect you're being boarded at night.

While bright lights in the right places are important, the liveaboard boat also needs a night-lighting system so navigation and food preparation can go on without blinding the helmsman. In crowded harbors, on narrow waterways, or when you're at sea searching for a reef or traffic, night vision must be zealously guarded. One or two red darkroom-type lights in the galley, one in the head, and one at the navigation station will let liveaboard routines go on. We also carry a couple of small flashlights which have optional red shades, for use underway at night.

Waterworks

Pressure water is almost taken for granted on most of today's boats, although there are still many who believe that pressure water means waste of water. People may waste water, but pumps do not. So you may as well have all the versatility, and economy of pressure water.

It's hard to control the amount of water you get from a manual pump, which gives you a measured plop of water each time. With a pressure system you can get a steady trickle of water to rinse soapy dishes or you can draw just a teaspoon of water for a recipe. Or let it rip, full blast, to fill the kettle in a hurry.

Once you have a pressure system aboard, you can have a shower, unlimited running water when you don't have to conserve, the option of hot water, and a plumbing system that can be hooked up to city water when you're at the dock. One pump can serve as many faucets as you need. You can add a cockpit shower, a foredeck washdown, even a wet bar if you wish.

The PAR diaphragm-type water pump aboard *Sans Souci* gave us ten years of quiet, trouble-free service. It drew 4.5 amps while pumping 1.8 gallons per minute at 20 pounds of pressure. If we drew 5.4 gallons per day—which was more than we drew even when we could be lavish with water—the pump ran a total of only three minutes per day. A reading lamp drawing one amp would use the same amount of current in only 13 minutes. At sea, when conserving both batteries and water, pump use was far less.

Of course, not all pressure systems need an electric pump. We saw a sailboat which had a five-gallon water tank inside the mast. This was filled as needed by a hand pump, and the water then gravity-fed to the galley and head sinks. One advantage of this feeder tank set-up is that you keep track of water use in small increments. Another boat, an older and deeper design, had water tanks under the cockpit seats— again high enough to provide gravity flow to the galley.

In designing your plumbing system, outline your present needs and then write to several pump manufacturers for literature. They'll explain how to choose a pump based on the number of outlets, maximum suction lift and discharge, and other factors. Then choose a pump one size larger, in case you want to add more outlets later.

This is also a good time to add tankage if possible. The more water you have on hand, the more independence you'll have. In the Bahamas, drinking water is sometimes expensive and of poor quality. Many areas of the world have unpotable water at dockside. In many parts of North America, city water tastes of sulphur or chlorine. The bigger your tanks, the more water you can take on when you find a plentiful, good-tasting source. Extra tankage is also handy for those liveaboards in the frozen north. Dockside water is turned off in winter because pipes would freeze, so tanks are filled only during thaws.

A filter to take out particulated matter should be incorporated in the system, and you may also want to add one of the new super filters that, according to the manufacturer, removes chemical and biological impurities. Such filters are good for only so-many gallons before a cartridge change is needed, so it's best to equip your sink with a special faucet. From that faucet, draw any water that is used for drinking and cooking. There's no point in filtering other water, since replacement cartridges are bulky to carry and expensive.

One reason why many boatbuilder-installed pressure systems provide a spasmodic flow is that the water goes directly from the pump to the faucet. Either buy a pump system which has a header tank (Raritan makes one), or build your own tank anywhere in the system you can find room for it. A header is simply a hollow air chamber that maintains a reservoir of pressure, evens out the flow, and keeps the pump from having to flick off and on with demand. Ours was made out of a length of 3-inch diameter PVC pipe. The larger the tank, the less often the pump has to run.

By adding a stainless steel, quick-disconnect deck fitting, and buying a white, taste-free water hose, we were able to plug our boat into city water anytime we were at the dock. You also need a valve that allows you to turn off this water in case a pipe breaks inside the boat, a hose-mounted water pressure reducer to avoid plumbing damage in

Raritan's water system has a built-in header tank. Commercial or home-made tanks give a more even water flow, and make your pressure water system work less hard.

If you have a deck fitting for your plumbing, you can easily change from tank water to city water.

Sink sprayer attached to a cockpit faucet with quick-release fitting is ideal for after-swim rinses.

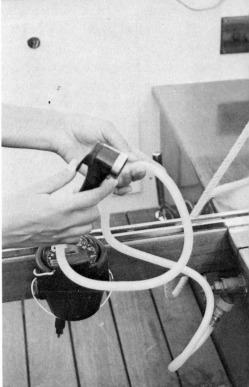

A garden sprayer can be filled with heated water and used as a shower on deck or below.

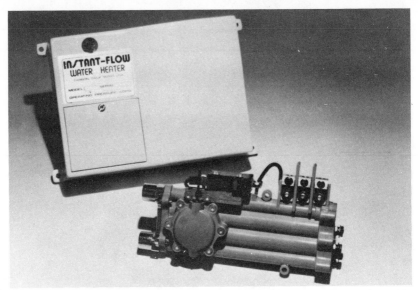

At-source water heaters like this one waste neither energy nor water but 110-volt power is needed.

Gas-fired water heaters like this one are common on European boats.

case the city water has a pressure surge, and a check valve to keep your tank water from being pumped overboard if you forget to close the deck valve after disconnecting city water. The deck fitting should also have a good cap, to keep out dirt and seawater.

There are a number of choices for your hot water system. The cheapest and easiest to install is an electric tank. It's probably the best choice if you have dock or generator power available. The Sears catalogue offers compact, ten-gallon, 110-220V household-type water heaters in several qualities starting at $80, including a super-insulated type that should hold many hours after you've turned off the generator. Raritan Engineering, 1025 N. High St., Millville, NJ 08332, sells electric six-and 12-gallon marine water heaters, with optional engine heat exchanger.

One source of bulkhead-mounted, instantaneous gas-fired water heaters is Gas Systems, 5361 Production Dr., Huntington Beach, CA 92649. You may have seen such at-source heaters on imported boats, and in homes and hotels if you've traveled abroad. Their drawback is that they serve just one faucet so you'll need one for the head and another for the galley.

Household-current, at-source water heaters come and go on the market, but one company which has been solidly in business for some time is Chronomite Laboratories, 21011 S. Figuera St., Carson, CA 90745. They make small 110V and 220V in-line water heaters which attach at the point of use. You can select 160-degree water for washing dishes, while setting the heater on the shower for a more comfortable 120 degrees. The heaters are compact, and are very economical on energy because they turn on only when you draw hot water. Prices begin at about $180. On the debit side, you can get hot water only when power is on, and you'll need one for each hot water faucet except in back-to-back installations.

The Galley Stove

Probably more curses have been flung, more questions asked, and more articles written about the marine stove than almost any other maritime topic. The stove is the heart and core of the galley. Almost every meal depends on it.

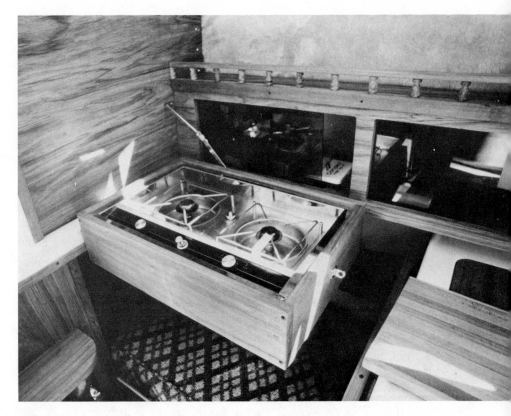

These three photos show a cooking stove on a small boat in its three different modes. First, the stove sits up above a berth, out of the way. Then, it becomes an extra counter, with chopping block. Finally it blossoms into a two-burner stove. Pretty good for a 25-foot boat.

Many fuels and types of stove are available, and I suggest getting more than one. We carried a one-burner electric stove (a Calrod unit, not a cheap, coil hotplate) which served in port as our electric skillet, percolator, waffle maker, corn popper, griddle, egg poacher, teakettle and every other countertop electric appliance, just by changing the pot on top.

Our seagoing stove, one we blessed at each meal and twice on days when we bought fuel, was a two-burner pressure kerosene Primus stove. It was hot, cheap, efficient, fume-free when used correctly, and we could buy kerosene easily in areas we cruised. A Sea Swing stove, fueled either with a Primus burner or Sterno, is a traditional favorite for rough-weather cooking. Another cooker liveaboards like is a barbecue because you can (1) cook outdoors on hot nights, (2) use a kettle barbecue to cook large roasts and turkeys which won't fit in small galley ovens, and (3) grill fish and steaks if your galley stove has no broiler. Kettle grills such as the Happy Cooker can also be used to smoke fish and meats. Just add a layer of wet wood chips to the charcoal. Coleman makes propane kettle cookers which can also be used to grill, roast, or smoke. A small, tabletop smoker that heats with either alcohol or Sterno is sold by Precision Sports, P. O. Box 219, Ithaca, NY 14850.

If you'll be dockside all the time, electric stoves are easy, clean, and pleasant to use. There are a couple of problems. One is that many docks aren't adequately wired for the big load put on them by electric stoves (especially in summer when everyone at the dock is also running air conditioning). Another is that 110-volt marine stoves aren't as quick as 220-volt kitchen stoves. Going to *sea* with an electric stove is another matter, and one Virgin Islands galley cook told me she was deep-sixing her beautiful ceramic cooktop in favor of a gas system because she was tired of starting and listening to the generator every time she wanted a cup of coffee. When you leave the dock you have a double chance of breakdown. The stove itself could pack up; so could the generator. Either way, you're out of business.

Microwave ovens are seen in many modern galleys today. The world divides into two camps on them, but I love mine and missed it terribly because there wasn't room in our telephone-booth-size gally for it.

They take up little room yet they can be used to thaw, quick-cook in hot weather, flash-cook a roast when you don't want to run the generator all day, make soggy crackers crisp again, reheat leftovers, and perform a million other menu miracles. If you have the space and the power capability, consider a microwave.

There are also two sides when it comes to gas stoves aboard. Some sailors wouldn't have propane aboard; some will have nothing else. The heat is hot, instant, clean, and inexpensive. The stoves are among the most economical in galley stoves because you can get a camper stove at camper (not yacht) prices. However, in world cruising, you have to carry a bouquet of adapters so your propane tanks can be filled in different countries. There is also the problem of getting the tanks off the boat, to the gas company for refilling, and back again.

One of the big questions about gas stoves has been safety, but the picture has changed a great deal in recent years. There are innumerable new safeguards such as solenoid shut-offs and bilge sniffers. Another safety factor is the increasing availability of lighter-than-air Compressed Natural Gas. For a list of places where CNG cylinders can be exchanged, and for information on how you can be supplied via common carriers, write GSI Gas Systems Inc., 5361 Production Dr., Huntington Beach, CA 92649.

Two types of stoves, coal/wood or diesel, should be considered by liveaboards in the Pacific Northwest, and other cool areas where extra heat in the galley is welcome all year. Diesel stoves are hot, inexpensive to run, and as pleasant to use as Grandma's old cookstove. When we cruised for a couple of weeks with friends who had a diesel stove, we liked the way the chimney heat was routed through a locker to keep crackers and cereals dry, and the way stove heat could be used to dry tea towels. The entire rangetop gets hot so the hottest areas over burners are used for quick cooking, more moderate areas for simmering, and cooler areas for warming plates. This stove used the same fuel you have aboard for your diesel engine, and they are wonderful bakers. Unfortunately, this cookstove was too hot for cooking in the tropics, where we happened to be at the time.

Many of the same things can be said of coal/wood cookstoves except that they are more difficult to start and regulate. Fuel is awkward to carry, and is dirty. Both diesel and coal/wood stoves are big and heavy, and need chimneys.

That leaves us with alcohol, which is the one galley stove fuel I don't recommend for anyone and especially for liveaboards. I once cruised for a week aboard a 41-footer which had an alcohol oven that could not be boosted above 200 degrees. Aboard other boats, I've lived with alcohol stoves, both pressure and non-pressure, and they were uniformly awful. Alcohol gives you less heat per dollar, per pound, and per gallon than anything else you can cook with except charcoal. Although it's touted as a "safe" fuel because alcohol fires can be extinguished with water, water dashed on a puddle of flaming alcohol can also spread the fire. It takes so long to cook a meal, compared to cooking with hotter fuels, that the open flame burns longer in your galley. And the flame is where the danger lies.

Over the years we've seen three boats burn to the waterline. Two of the fires started in the galley, and both were in stoves considered safest—electric and alcohol. Anything that starts fires is dangerous, and any stove fuel is only as safe as the people and equipment associated with it.

Refrigeration

The biggest and best refrigerator you can get for the money is a household type. With it you can get automatic defrost, an automatic ice maker, and other luxury features all for the price of a much smaller, more spartan, non-household unit. If you'll be living at the dock fulltime, or plan to run a generator at all times, a kitchen refrigerator is by far the best choice. The problem is that these refrigerators aren't meant to be turned off, even for a few hours a day, so they need fulltime power availability. The exception is a well-filled household freezer, which can keep food in the tropics with four hours of generator time in the morning, four hours more at night.

It's when sailors leave the dock that all sorts of silliness takes over. Cruising sailors may shatter the benign Bahamas quiet with hours of deafening noise from portable generators. One couple ran their engine, at anchor, four hours a day to charge the batteries which were powering a tiny, 12-volt icebox containing a sixpack of beer. Countless cruising families plan their entire lives around when they need ice and where they can get it. We visited a boatyard where a very costly, round-the-world sailboat was nearing completion. The entire galley was filled with a huge freezer, yet there were hardly any drawers or lockers for other stores.

You can eat well without a refrigerator, freezer, or ice. We did for months at a time, and the story is told in my *The Galley Book* ($12 ppd. from Botebooks, Box 248, DeLeon Springs, FL 32028) and in my *Cooking on the Go* ($13.95 in book stores or from Sail Books, 34 Commercial Wharf, Boston, MA 02100).

Our boat had a well-insulated icebox which a previous owner had equipped with a 110-volt Grunert holding-plate system. It was ideal for the day cruising that the family did because it cooled down all night, then held for up to 24 hours until the boat was plugged in again. The unit was at least 15 years old when we sold *Sans Souci* and it had never given us a moment's trouble even though, when we left to cruise the Bahamas, it wasn't used for six months at a time.

Eutectic or "holding" plates with engine-driven compressors are the primary choice today of those cruising sailors who want the most refrigeration for the least fuel use. Grunert and Adler-Barbour both make fine systems. Howard Crosby, who founded Crosby Refrigeration Systems, not only makes a superb, reliable system, he'll sell you an indispensable book on refrigeration theory and practice. Crosby's address is 204 Second Ave. S., St. Petersburg, FL 33701.

If you do select an engine-driven system, get a system which will also work on dockside power. It isn't fair to your marina neighbors to run the engine every day just to power your refrigeration, nor is it an efficient use of engine life and fuel.

There are other conversion units available for an icebox. Some are compressor types and others are solid state units that transfer heat silently, using little electricity, by putting current across dissimilar metals. All are seen at boat shows and in marine catalogues. Such conversion units require fulltime 110-volt or 12-volt power. The better insulated your icebox, the more efficient they will be.

In addition to household readymades there are also those refrigerators and refrigerator-freezer units made for recreational vehicles.

Some work on either 110-volt or 12-volt power. Some will work on propane too, and are a silent and economical choice for many boats, particularly houseboats on which you can rig an outside exhaust. Like household units they are mass produced so price (while higher than kitchen-type appliances) is attractive compared to custom installations. They can be removed easily from the boat for service, and parts are readily available.

One problem with any of the household units is that their discharge heat ends up in the galley. With a custom unit, exhaust heat can be routed to the engine room or into an underwater heat sink.

This Norcold unit has a compressor. It can be used as a refrigerator or as a zero-degree freezer and works on both 110-volt or 12-volt power. It can hold up to 25 pounds of food.

The biggest drawback to having mechanical refrigeration after you leave the dock is that there are so many ways you can lose it. The refrigeration system, with its complicated lash-up of wires and tubing, could break down. The engine could fail, which means you can't run the compressor or charge the batteries. And when you're out of the water for bottom paint and repairs, where most liveaboards spend at least a few days each year, you can't use a system that depends on an underwater heat sink or water cooling.

Whatever your choice of refrigerator or freezer, I recommend fitting yours with a thermometer on the outside, and a probe inside so you can monitor temperatures any time without opening the door. The safety of fresh food depends on keeping it below 45 degrees F or 10 degrees C. Frozen food keeps best at zero. When you are trying to skimp on battery or generator use, you risk food poisoning if foods are not kept cold enough.

Curtains

To the homeowner, curtains may be just part of the decor but to the liveaboard curtains provide needed insulation, they keep the sun from fading upholstery and brightwork below, and they are the only way to gain privacy in crowded marinas. Aboard your boat, you need curtains that close tightly to keep out prying eyes and sunbeams, fabrics that will hold up against bright sun and constant motion, and a style that will be both attractive and practical.

My favorite curtain fabric is a white, medium-weight cotton blend that is thick enough to be opaque when the lights are on below at night yet thin enough to allow full brightness below during the day even when the curtains are closed. White doesn't fade in the sun and it can be bleached if it stains or mildews. It also makes the boat bright below even when closed. If you want more sun filtering, line any curtains or drapes with a fabric called Milium, which reflects light. If you're buying decorator fabrics, read labels. Most have to be dry cleaned, and are not as colorfast as washables.

Curtain rods can be simple lengths of brass rod or wood dowel. Curtains can be attached with wood, plastic, or brass rings. There are also commercial curtain "systems" on the market, which combine

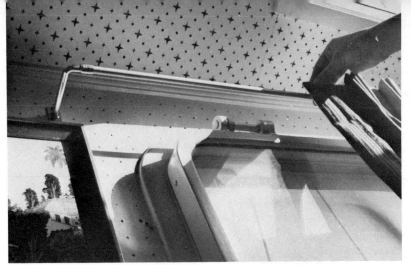

When you're making curtain rods, be sure to allow room for the depth of thick ports, and don't use plated metal rods, because they will rust quickly.

This grabrail doubles as a curtain tie-back.

This wheelhouse window has a slat shade on a spring roller. The pull-ring secures to a hook on the bottom.

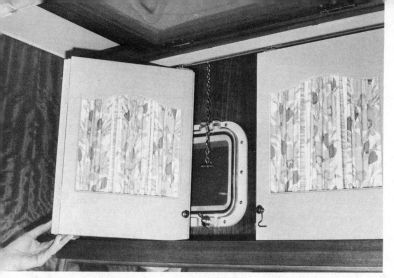

These frames with fabric in the center admit a very homey light. They operate on a track and don't sway in a seaway.

In this pilothouse the curtains are shaped to extend forward to the windshield, and held taut by snaps.

This is a simple tube of material stretched by two curtain rods.

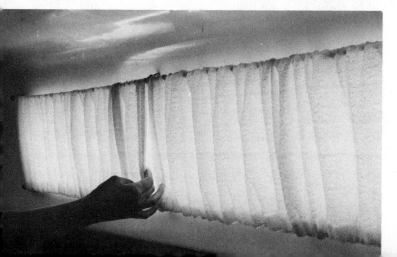

plastic and Velcro for curtains which are easy to slide open and closed. They're advertised in boating magazines and are sold in marine stores and catalogues. Avoid department-store-type fixtures unless you're sure they won't rust or corrode. Brass-coated or painted steel household-type rods and hooks will rust quickly in salt air, and soon enough even if you live aboard in fresh water.

Have some way to hold curtains closed if you're living cheek by jowl in a marina and don't want the neighbors to inventory your after-dark activities. At the same time, you also need sturdy tiebacks to keep curtains open and, more important, from flopping and waving underway. The motion not only wears the fabric, it is distracting to anyone below and is sure to start seasickness in those who are prone.

The photos show some ideas in curtain design.

Stereo and TV

For many of us, music and television are a part of everyday life. Thanks to today's fine selection of 12-volt TV's and automotive stereo systems, it's possible to have topnotch entertainment aboard at very little cost.

Our cassette stereo system, bought at an automotive supply store, was a roaring success despite its small speakers, because the shape of the hull served as an ideal sound chamber. If you often have guests or relatives aboard, a good use for the stereo is for privacy. At bedtime, you can play the stereo for an hour, loud enough to cover the sounds of whatever bickering or wooing might be going on in both cabins. A sound idea.

If you'll be using a TV on battery power most of the time, a black and white television will use much less power than color. Recreational vehicle supply stores sell folding TV antennas, including some that have a separate mount. The mount can be installed on the boat; the antenna put away until it's needed.

The new video cassette recorders are great entertainment for those who can afford them. There were two aboard a luxurious new Fead-ship motor yacht in Fort Lauderdale. The lucky owners will always have television, even when they are well outside the range of station signals. If you're on a very modest budget and will be cruising so widely

This 46-foot houseboat is home for a family of four. One of the kids, aged 15, is a computer whiz, and can practice right at home at the dock. His screen is on the right.

you don't care to carry a TV set, I recommend taking one of the little portable radios that pulls in TV sound. When you are in other countries you can learn a lot by listening to radio; even more by listening to, even if you cannot watch, television.

Electronics

As a liveaboard you are one of the few people who has no telephone unless you stay at the same dock long enough to justify the expense of having one installed. Because you have no telephone, you may want more and different communication radios than the boating vacationer.

The most useful tool for keeping in touch with your family, broker, suppliers, and fellow boating families is ham radio. It's always there, in port or at sea, every hour of the day or night. There are several "nets" for cruising sailors, and the information you get about weather, navigating in uncharted waters, and up-to-date scoop on politically unstable countries can save your life. Fellow hams will also patch in telephone links for you with your family back home.

If you're at the dock long enough, a phone hook-up can be installed, see upper left. Notice that this phone is a cordless model.

Cordless phone, shown in previous photograph, in use.

The wind instruments and running rigging are right alongside the electrical and phone hook-ups.

Strict laws govern the use of these radios, and you may need extensive training (including learning Morse code) plus licenses. If you have a ham radio club in your town, start there, or write the American Radio Relay League, 225 Main St., Newington, CT 06111.

VHF is the main marine communications radio and you need single sideband radio for longer range. Such phone calls are very expensive but are your only way to keep in touch with a business back home since ham radio can't be used for commercial purposes.

In many areas, CB radio is more important than VHF for marine and social messages. Its range, however, is very limited. It's widely used in the Abaco area of the Bahamas and in many areas of the States. And, when you're cruising a long, lonely river such as the Ohio or the Mississippi, the CB can link you with people ashore, as well as other boats.

Shore Power Wiring

Although there are people who live aboard for years without ever using shore power, most liveaboards will be at dock at least part of the time. Since power is included in the price of most dockage, you may as well have your boat wired with plenty of outlets, so you can use 110-volt appliances while you're plugged in. Even aboard our tiny 29-footer, we carried hair clippers, a hair dryer, electric razor, blender, mixer, heater, fans, hot plate, water heater, vacuum cleaner, trouble light, soldering iron, electric drill, saber saw, electric typewriter, and a battery charger—all of which worked on shore power.

Although some of the appliances also worked on our small Heathkit inverter (which converts 12-volt battery power to 110-volt, most couldn't be used for months at a time while we cruised. Yet we found it more than worthwhile to have them aboard. Thanks to the 110-volt wiring throughout *Sans Souci* we were able to use all these conveniences in port without tangled skeins of lead cords all over the boat.

For information on safely wiring your boat for 110-volt service, order booklet E-8 which is $6 from the American Boat and Yacht Council, P.O. Box 806, Amityville, NY 11701. The Council is a non-profit organization which sets standards for boat manufacture, outfitting, and repair.

To find equipment for your liveaboard boat, shop at boat shows, marine stores, camping stores, and marine catalogues. Both *Yachting* and *Sail* magazines publish annual equipment directories listing manufacturers of various gear.

Free catalogues include:

L.L. Bean, Casco St., Freeport, ME 04033.

Camping World, P.O. Box S, Bowling Green, KY 42101.

Crook & Crook, 2804 Bird Rd., Miami, FL 33133.

E&B Marine Supply Inc., 150 Jackson Ave., Edison, NJ 08818.

Goldberg's Marine, 202 Market St., Philadelphia, PA 19106.

Jay Stuart Haft, 2925 N. Tennyson Dr., Milwaukee, WI 53217.

Manhattan Marine, 116 Chambers St., New York, NY 10017.

Sears camping and Sears boating catalogues, available at Sears Roebuck stores.

Tom Taylor Co., 136 Adelaide St., E., Toronto, Ontario, Canada.

If you'll be doing much of your outfitting by mail, you might like to read David Kendall's *Shopping at Home for Boat Equipment* (Dolphin Book Club or in book stores), $9.95 paper $15.95 hardback.

There are many things that make a boat a home: knickknacks from a voyage, favorite books at hand, and a comfortable pillow.

Chapter **5**

To Quit or to Keep

∾∾∾

W hat do furniture storage or garage sales have to do with living on a boat? A lot, if your present possessions mean anything to you financially, sentimentally, even socially.

Some family belongings are beyond price. You don't want to sell them so you have to store them or give them away. Any way you choose can lead to hard feelings. If you give the monogrammed linens to your sister, your brother's wife will feel slighted because it is her children who bear the family name. If you let Phyllis and Carl keep the silver service for you, there will be trouble if it is stolen from them or lost in a fire. If Uncle Angus volunteers to make room for the big oak sideboard, you're stuck for a big moving bill when he accepts a new job 1,500 miles away, and another big hauling bill to get the sideboard back when you come finally to roost somewhere.

One couple solved the problem of family things by giving all their closest relatives an equal amount of Monopoly money and letting them "buy" family pieces which had been professionally appraised. Those that weren't claimed by anyone could then be sold with a clear conscience.

Once family heirlooms are placed you still have to decide what to do with everything else—some of it nearly worthless, some achingly dear to you, some of it valuable enough to pay for a year of cruising. We sold almost everything, left a few things with each set of parents, and found friends back in Illinois who volunteered to keep the china and a couple of big antiques we just couldn't bear to sell. I don't know how binding it was legally, but we gave our friends a signed paper, absolving

81

~~~~~~

them of responsibility and willing them the things if we died before reclaiming them. It all worked out beautifully, but then these friends were very special people.

We decided to sell through the want ads, starting with things we seldom used. The slide projector, bicycles, and guest room furniture were advertised and shown by appointment. In the weeks that followed, Gordon finished the water tank and other major items he had made for the boat and we were then ready to sell his large shop tools. The living room, dining room, and Porsche were sold—all through individual ads and by appointment. We weren't able to handle hordes of bargain seekers yet.

During the last three weeks before we vacated the house, we advertised large items during the week, showing them only by appointment because we didn't want people wandering through the house. On weekends, we had garage sales. Luckily, we had a large garage where things could be locked up until opening time, sheltered from sun and rain, and sold in a controlled space. The crowds were crushing. We were lucky, and had only a few very minor shoplifting incidents. I do not recommend letting such mobs into the house.

Among the other things we learned from our garage sales:

1.   Don't give in when people come to the sale ahead of your advertised time. We were besieged by people who came at dawn or even the night before. Early in the garage-sale game you're so anxious to get on with it that the buyer is king. However, we reasoned that we weren't so desperate that we had to have our lives interrupted this way. Besides, it wasn't fair to those people who did come during the advertised hours. It turned out that we didn't suffer from any sales we may have lost by refusing these early birds.

2.   Have some sort of crowd control. If you don't have a porch or garage to contain your sale, put up snow fencing or ropes or some other device for keeping people from wandering in and out of the yard at will.

3.   Have plenty of bags and boxes on hand.

4.   Put a price on everything. We used masking tape.

5.   Get lots of change ahead of time, and have a way to handle all

the cash you'll be taking in. While the cigar box is fine for smaller garage sales, we were too busy to keep an eye on a cash box. We each wore carpenter aprons with change in one pocket, bills in a clip in the other. The house was left locked, and from time to time we took some bills inside so we wouldn't have large rolls in our pockets.

6.   Try to attend several garage sales or flea markets before you start selling out, to get an idea of what your things are worth. If you haven't shopped secondhand stores you'll be surprised at the high prices, and if you've been keeping house for ten years or more you may be amazed to find that many things can be sold for more than you paid for them.

7.   Consider giving some things away if you can't get top dollar for them. We weren't able to get even $5 for expensive business suits, and books wouldn't even sell for a dollar. So we donated them, got receipts for their real worth, and wrote them off on our income tax.

8.   If you have a really large household, as we did, plan on several garage sales and don't put everything out at first. We had sales three weekends in a row, and some customers came to all three. This gave us a smaller, more manageable inventory each time but with some exciting new items to lure new buyers. Each time someone asked us to take less than our asking price, we stood firm but invited them to come back on the final afternoon. Only then did we begin slashing prices. By then, most things had sold at our prices.

The last things to go were the washer and dryer, followed by our bedroom set and the kitchen appliances. I sat down in the middle of the bare living room carpet and had a good cry. It had been withering to see the treasures of a lifetime appraised, rejected, bargained for, and carried away—by strangers. Deciding what to keep and what to sell had been emotionally wearing, and I was exhausted from the physical work of lugging things to the garage and then dealing with wave after wave of bargain hunters.

Auctions

One way to keep from spending the time and emotional wear and tear of selling your life piecemeal is to call in an auctioneer. We have met some liveaboards who chose this route and never regretted it. If you have a yard large enough for the crowds and for parking their cars, you can have it right at the house. Otherwise the auction house trucks things away, to be sold at their regular auctions. The auctioneer does all the advertising and promotion, carries things out into the yard, gets the best prices possible, and turns over to you a check for 65 to 75% of the proceeds.

The good thing about an auction is that you don't have to be there to see your precious possessions melt away. The work is done for you, and some liveaboards have felt that they got better prices than they would have any other way. On the minus side, there is that hefty chunk taken by the auctioneer and the chance that your auction will be held on the wrong day. Weather could be bad, there could be too many competing auctions, or the season could be all wrong to attract big bidders.

Secondhand Dealers

Unless you're utterly desperate, I don't recommend letting a second-hand dealer buy your household goods. We called in several, who gave bids that were simply laughable. The advantage to this method is that it is quick and involves no physical work, no investment in advertising, and no contact with the public. We have had somewhat better luck with consignment houses. You take them your furniture, set your price, and wait for them to do the selling. When and if the item sells, they keep a percentage (we paid 25%).

Storage

There are several different types and qualities of furniture storage, and one of them might be right for you, especially if you plan to live aboard for only a specified length of time and if you'll be returning to the same town. On the minus side are high cost, expense of moving everything later if you decide to settle down in San Diego rather than returning to Indiana, deterioration in storage, and the very real tug you feel when you're beating to windward and thinking about that cozy wing chair just waiting for you back in the warehouse.

Mini-warehouses have sprung up all over America because so many of us now live in apartments, condo's, and in homes which have no attics or basements. In our area you can get a 4 × 4 × 8-foot cubbyhole for about $12 per month. You put your own lock on the door and go into the storage space any time you care to during hours when the facility is open. Security is fairly good because such warehouse complexes are usually fenced and have a night guard, dogs, or alarms. This locker does not have electricity, however, so you can't use a dehumidifier.

At the upper end of the scale, this same central Florida warehouse offers a 10 × 22 ×8-foot room, with its own garage-type door, for about $65 a month. This includes electricity for running your own dehumidifier or fan. Prices may differ in your part of the country.

For full household storage the price is high, but it may be worth it to you if you want to take up housekeeping again someday just where you left off. One of the large, national moving and storage companies quoted a 1982 price of $1.25 per hundredweight (cwt.) per month for storage and a mandatory $1.50 cwt. per month for insurance which covers 60 cents per pound per article. If you want additional insurance, it is 85 cents per $1,000 value per month. In addition, you pay $5 per cwt. to have the furniture moved from your home to the storehouse. For the average furnishings stored locally this amounts to about $50 per room. When you want to reclaim the furniture, you then pay current moving costs to have it taken out of the warehouse and brought to you.

Let's say you have four rooms of furniture valued at $10,000. Experts guess that the average room weighs 750-1,000 pounds, so if we take 4,000 pounds × $2.75 cwt, your monthly cost with the mandatory insurance would be $110. Your goods are insured for 60 cents per pound, or $2,400. If you want to insure for the full $10,000, at 85 cents per 1,000 pounds, budget an additional $8.50 per month. You'll also have the initial, and final, hauling charges. Prices, of course, will vary according to company and area.

At the central-Florida company that gave us this quote, you get a bonded warehouse with sprinkler system and circulating fans. Your goods are put in vault-type containers so they are separate from other stored furnishings. Large items such as sofas are put on special racks where they get full air circulation.

"Still, it's important to put things away clean," we were told by this storage expert. "If your upholstered furniture and carpeting are stained even slightly, the stains will deepen and set in storage. We can't guarantee that things won't rust and mildew."

Some combination of the various storage methods may be best for you, as it was for us. When you deal with a professional storage company you have specified protection (which varies with the company) and you're not causing inconvenience to friends or relatives. On the other hand, you may want to leave some personal items with a trusted friend or relative. If you're cruising somewhere and need a document or your down-filled vest, or if you run short of money and decide to sell the flatware, a friend or relative can root around your belongings, find what you want, and do what you want with it. A warehouse cannot.

During our three-month shakedown cruise, we left our van at the boatyard where we had outfitted. Some surplus goods were left in it. But then, fully committed to the liveaboard life, we decided to sell our last link to the land. For the next couple of years everything was on board with us. Then, when it became apparent that we'd do our hauling and recommissioning at the same boatyard each year, we rented one of their storage lockers. It was only $5 a month for a chicken wire cage inside a locked room. Security was not good, since other locker renters also had the key to the room, but it was just the space we needed to stow the extra gear that one accumulates.

Summing up: whether you decide to sell or to store, weigh each option carefully. Possessions can be a very expensive anchor. Except for occasional twinges for the Tom Lehrer records or the well-broken-in army boots, we've been very glad we sold out as mercilessly as we did. If we had it to do over, we'd sell out again.

Chapter 6

Keeping Warm, Keeping Cool

Think for a minute about the amount of space in your house that is devoted to furnace, stove, fireplace, air conditioners, and all the ducting necessary to transport cold or hot air through your home and to conduct smoke and dangerous fumes outside. Much of the bulk is behind the scenes in the chimney, attic, and basement, but in your boat there is little backstage room to spare. We once spent a few weeks aboard a borrowed sailboat that had central heating. Every time I opened a locker to stow something, I found it filled with fat hoses for the heating system. The heater itself was only about the size of a household vacuum cleaner, but the ductwork cost this boat owner most of his smaller lockers and parts of many of his larger stowage areas.

While central heat and air conditioning are nice to have no matter where you live, compromises have to be made on a boat. Much depends, of course, on where you live. In the Pacific Northwest and in the wonderful far-northern cruising areas of Lake Superior, northern Europe, Nova Scotia, and Maine, heat is needed even in summer. I remember shivering through one cold, rainy 4th of July in Nova Scotia, when the high temperature for the day was 12 degrees C.

Those people who winter aboard in freezing climates have special needs. In addition to a dependable, effective heating system, you also need a "bubbler" to keep the water around you from freezing. Various bubbler/de-icer devices are sold by Air-O-Later, 8100 Paseo, Kansas City, MO 64131; Hinde Engineering, 654 Deerfield Rd., Highland Park, IL 60035; Kasco Marine, 16065 32nd. St., S. Alton MN 55001;

Marland Environmental Systems, 27 N. Main St., Walworth, WI 53184; Powerhouse, 2662 W. Patapsco, Baltimore, MD 21231; Dick Scott & Co., 1826 Ottawa Beach Rd., Holland, MI 49423; and Unarco Industries, Box 2000, Peoria, IL 61656.

Northern liveaboards need plenty of tankage for drinking water because dockside water pipes must be turned off in winter. First, choose a dark color for your hull so it will absorb as much of the sun's warmth as possible. When we changed our deck color from blue to white, it was 15 degrees cooler down below on sunny days in the tropics. On the cold, brilliantly sunny days that Florida has after the passage of a cold front, we could make it warmer down below by covering hatches with black plastic garbage bags. If you live aboard in a very cold area, make use of the sun's heat by using heat-absorbent colors or go further by adding a solar heating system. There are instructions in Pat Rand Rose's *Solar Boat Book* which is $10.45 ppd. from Aqua-Sol, P.O. Box 340968, Miami, FL 33134. Northern liveaboards also find it pays

A clean, well-organized engine room is a blessing on any boat. A hot water heater and air conditioning system are in this one.

to cover as much of the boat as can conveniently be "tented." Consult a canvas expert about a cover that will stand up to whipping winter winds and snow loads as it provides insulation.

Most of us, however, live aboard in moderate, if not downright steamy, parts of the world. No matter where you live aboard there will be days when you'd like to be cooler or warmer and we all have several needs in common. The heating and/or cooling system must be safe, and free of fire danger and noxious fumes. It should be efficient, making optimum use of whatever wind or fuel or dockside hook-up you have. It should be highly effective. Boats are, by nature, poorly insulated. You need more heater/air conditioner capacity than you think. And, the system should not add to the woes of dampness which you already have. Combustion (charcoal, kerosene, wood, diesel stoves) adds moisture to the boat unless you have a proper chimney; electric heat is dry but expensive and sometimes unavailable.

Heating
Portables Versus Built-ins
Among electric, catalytic, and diesel/kerosene wick heaters, some are available in both portable and permanent types. The advantage to portables is that they can be banished to a shoreside storage locker in summer. In use, they can be placed or aimed anywhere heat is needed, to make the most use of the least heat. They can easily be tossed off the boat for repair or replacement, they are generally inexpensive, and you can take yours elsewhere with you if you go camping or rent a cabin when vacationing off your boat.

The advantage to built-ins is that they can be vented outdoors without the massive heat loss you have when you run a portable that requires an open hatch for fresh air. If they are installed properly they can be used underway. They are always with you so you don't have to go scrambling in the storage locker for a heater if there is an unexpected cold snap.

Heat From Air Conditioners
There are a number of choices for boats (see air conditioners) and many models have a heating cycle of some type. The advantage here is that one unit does double duty. The heat is dry and without worrisome

gases. Don't rely on this as your sole source of heating unless you winter south of, say, Charleston. I've never seen an air conditioner which is as effective a furnace as it was a chiller. Still, heat from your air conditioner is an ideal answer if you need only occasional, supplemental heat.

Electric Heaters

The advantage to this quick, dry heat is that you have a very large choice of mass-produced household units at discount store prices. While care is needed in using electric heaters, good ones turn off automatically if they tip over. Both radiant and forced-air types are available, and in many sizes. A heater the size of a cigar box, with a built-in fan, was always aboard with us even though we could use it only when we had shore-power hook-up. The heat was adequate for our 29-foot boat during Florida winters when temperatures sometimes plunged into the high 20's. Household-type electric baseboard heating is inexpensive and easy to install on houseboats and is efficient enough for the coldest climates.

However, household heaters will rust out eventually in damp salt air. Also, you'll be without heat if your power source (shore power, generator) fails or if voltage isn't adequate for this high-draw item. Many liveaboards running many electric heaters on the end of a long cord add up to too little heat for everyone.

Two companies which make portable electric heaters specifically for the marine market are Aquadynamics, 168 Rockland, Woonsocket, RI 02895 and Intermatic Inc., Intermatic Plaza, Spring Grove, IL 60081.

Wood, Charcoal, and Coal

There is nothing cozier than a crackling fire, and some very attractive little stove and fireplace units are made especially for boat use. The greater your need for heat, the larger the stove you need. Wood and diesel cookstoves double as heaters in many boats. If you have a free source of wood—driftwood or boatyard scraps, for example—you have free heat independent of dockside power. And your heating stove is a back-up for cooking in case your cookstove fails.

On the minus side, stoves and fireplaces do take up space—space you may not want to give up if you live in a hot climate and need a fire only occasionally. They're permanently installed, and can't be off-

A large diesel heater has its own foredeck locker on this 46-footer, shared with the large storm anchor.

loaded during the summer as portables can be. Wood, coal, and charcoal are bulky to stow and messy to use. On a long, cold passage you could carry more BTU's in less space with diesel oil or kerosene. You'll need a chimney, which means another hole in the boat, and you'll have to stay on guard against fires and fumes.

Sources of solid fuel stoves and heaters include Paul E. Luke, E. Boothbay, ME 04544; Shipmate, Richmond Ring, Box 375, Souderton, PA 18964; and Washington Stove Works, Box 687, Everett, WA 98206.

Oil Heating

If your engine uses diesel fuel, it's convenient to use diesel for heating, too. Both portable and built-in diesel heaters are sold, and they provide a hot, efficient, low-cost heat. There is also a wide choice of portable kerosene heaters, newly popular with home owners who are trying to save on fuel costs. We have, for instance, an Aladdin Lassie model radiant heater that puts out 10-12,000 BTUs per hour, heats an area 20 feet square, and burns up to 20 hours on one and a half gallons of kerosene. It has automatic ignition (two D-cell batteries), and it turns off automatically if it upsets.

The disadvantage to all oil heaters is that they put moisture in the air, they do have some odor, and they have to be vented in some way. Built-ins can be equipped with permanent venting and most can be used underway. When you're using a portable you have to assure some flow of fresh air and it would be unwise to use one in a seaway unless you have a very secure spot for it.

A small 12-volt fan circulates warm air from the kerosene heater, or, in the summer, it blows cool air around the cabin.

Sources include Dickinson Marine Products, 4300-11th Ave., Seattle, WA 98107; Espar Products, 6480 Viscount Rd., Mississauga, Ontario, Canada L4V 1H3; Faire Harbor, 4 Captain Pierce Rd., Scituate, MA 02066; Force 10 Marine, 4-8100 River Rd., Richmond B.C., Canada; Jay Stuart Haft, 2925 N. Tennyson Dr., Milwaukee, WI 53217; Johnson & Joseph, 76 Jack London Sq., Oakland, CA 94606; Kero-Sun, P.O. Box 540, Kent, CT 06757; ALH Inc., P.O. Box 10025, Nashville, TN 37210 (Aladdin heaters); Marine Heat, 4400 23rd Ave. W., Seattle, WA 98199; Marine Parts NW, 817 Republican St., Seattle, WA 98109; Shipmate Stove Division, Richmond Ring, P.O. Box 375, Souderton, PA 18964; Washington Stove Works, Box 687, Everett, WA 98206; Way-Wolff Associates, 45-10 Vernon Blvd., Long Island City, NY 11101. Also see local Sears stores or the Sears Boating and Fishing catalogue.

Catalytic Heaters

They're sold in almost every camping, fishing, and sporting goods store. Like electrics, catalytics are a lowcost, mass-produced, flameless, portable heater—except that you need no electricity. Coleman, one of the leading manufacturers of camping heaters, makes three catalytics. The smallest puts out 3,500 BTUs and holds two quarts of Coleman fuel; the largest holds six quarts and is rated for 8,000 BTUs J.C. Whitney Company (P.O. Box 8410, Chicago, IL 60680) sells a portable model, a catalytic heater which can be permanently installed, and a roof-mount, flameless heater which is designed for recreational vehicles but which would fit many types of boats. Allcraft (55 Border St., West Newton, MA 02165) sells a propane-fired catalytic.

Disadvantages to catalytics include fumes. We once spent a freezing week on the Thames in October, desperately needing the portable catalytic heater which was provided, but smarting from the smells. Portables must be used with adequate ventilation (and attendant heat loss), and you may have to carry a special fuel.

Propane Furnace

Propane furnaces are used almost universally in recreational vehicles. If you have gas aboard anyway and a safe way of venting it, an efficient, inexpensive propane trailer furnace may be just the answer for your boat-home. Houseboats are particularly well suited to this type of installation. Propane is easily available, fairly inexpensive, hot, clean, and less odiferous than many other fuels.

However, propane is an explosive fuel and must be used with caution—especially on a boat. You'll need a large supply of it to get you through a cold winter on a boat, which means frequent trips to refill tanks. Propane is only rarely sold dockside. You need adequate venting to be safe from carbon monoxide. Trailer-type furnaces take their combustion air from outside, so they don't deplete oxygen indoors. While a propane furnace can save you from reliance on quantities of shore power, you will need either a 110-volt or 12-volt blower.

A common household thermostat regulates this boat's propane heat.

Catalytic heaters are sold widely in sporting goods stores.

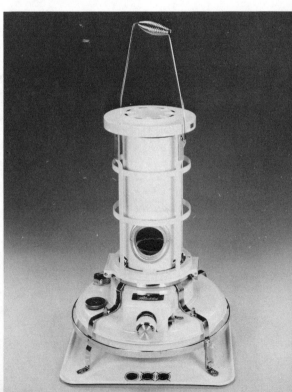

Many a boat is kept warm in winter by an Aladdin kerosene heater.

A variety of radiant and convection kerosene portable heaters is available. Portables provide quick, efficient, inexpensive heat but they have their drawbacks.

Engine Heat Exchange

Although I don't know of any manufacturer offering a boat heater that relies on engine heat, I have seen several custom installations. If your boat is fresh-water cooled, and if you'll be underway a great deal, you can heat your boat with the many thousands of throw-away BTUs your engine produces. Basically, you need a heater coil to loop engine-cooling water into the boat, and a blower to distribute heat from these coils into the living quarters. You can cobble up the installation from auto parts if you're handy. Or, J.C. Whitney (address above) sells a readymade unit that includes a blower, grillwork and housing, and optional thermostatic control.

The disadvantage to using engine heat for your cabin is that you have heat only when the engine is running. If this is your only heating system, and you have to run the engine sometimes for heating alone, it's a very inefficient way to use fuel and your engine's lifespan. Like the heater in your car, this one contains water that is often at near-boiling temperatures so a proper installation is mandatory.

Cooling

Air Conditioning

There are three major choices among mechanical air conditioning units for your boat. You can buy a household window unit and find a way to mount it in an existing hatch and/or cut a hole just for this purpose. you can roof-mount a recreational vehicle air conditioner in a suitable hatch. Almost all houseboats use them. Or, you can choose among those marine air conditioners which are engineered specifically for boats.

Household, Window-Mount Air Conditioners

These are inexpensive because they are mass-produced. Most brands have a long history of dependability, and, if you do have trouble with a national brand, repairs and parts are easily available throughout North America and the Caribbean. And you can easily tote one off the boat and to the repairman. No space is robbed from your down-below living area because a window unit hangs outdoors. The disadvantage to these units is that they are not very yachty and can, in fact, be downright ugly. They aren't constructed to go to sea, so will corrode quickly in salt air. They are noisy, they blow all their cool air into one spot, and they deposit the waste heat on deck. They are still, however, a very logical choice for dockside liveaboards.

Recreational Vehicle Air Conditioners

These offer somewhat more to the boating family. They mount overhead, usually in an existing hatch, and spill cool air into the cabin in a flow pattern that I find more comfortable than that of a window unit. While they are more expensive than window units, they are less expensive than custom, marine units. The styling is sleek, sportier than a boxy window unit, and weather resistant (although these too will be destroyed by long-time salt abuse). Like window units, these portables can be removed from the boat fairly easily for service and, because the major brands are sold so widely for RV use, parts and service will be easy to find. Like window units, they mount outdoors so don't take space from your living area. We have a 12,000 BTU Coleman rooftop air conditioner on our motorhome, and it has given us 12 years of troublefree service.

Disadvantages of rooftop air conditioners include noise. We call ours The Screamer. Hot air is discharged on deck, which is a problem if someone is working or sunbathing there. Like window units, they constantly drip condensation, so you have to make sure this water drips overboard immediately. If it collects anywhere where it can penetrate wood, rot will result. They are heavy and they vibrate, which could be a problem if you mount yours where such stresses were not allowed for by the designer.

Marine Air Conditioners

The third, most expensive, and most comfortable air conditioner for your boat-home is one designed just for the liveaboard. It is installed below, safe from the elements. Discharge heat will go into the water, not the air around you. Condensate, in a proper unit, will be channeled harmlessly into a bilge or sump. Air flow, in a good installation, will be quiet and free of drafts.

Among marine air conditioners there are some basic controversies. Some manufacturers make free-standing units; others make modular units. Some promote chilled-water air conditioning in which pipes must be run throughout the boat to carry cold water which cools the air that passes over it. Others promote what is called a direct expansion method. I've used the word "controversies" because, in talking to salesmen at boat shows, I've often been blitzed with doubletalk, doublethink, evasions, and outright lies. It's a subject that gets a lot of people very hot under the collar for some reason. I've brought all this up because you may have to do a lot of research to find the marine air conditioner that will be best for you, wade through a lot of banana oil, and stand up to one or two salesmen. One, for instance, looked Gordon and me up and down and sniffed, "We don't make anything smaller than five tons." Clearly, he was telling us to buzz off so he'd have more time for folks who looked more affluent than we do.

In shopping for a marine air conditioner there are a couple of stumbling blocks. One is that *boat* salesmen may talk you into too small an air conditioner capacity because they're trying to keep the overall boat price as low as possible. I've been aboard a dozen boats on which there was factory-installed air, and none of them was comfortable until after the sun went down.

Decide where and how you want to use the air conditioner. If you'll be outdoors all day, enjoying the sun and water, and want air conditioning only for cool sleeping at night, you can make do with a smaller unit. If, however, you live aboard in the tropics and will be working and cooking aboard during the day, you need far more than you'd choose for a house or room of comparable size ashore. Even more cooling power will be needed if your boat has a lot of window area. If you are in cold water and hot air, your needs will be less than that of the family in hot air and hot water. An expert who understands both boats and air conditioning is your best guide.

Among the major manufacturers of marine air conditioning, most offer you a choice of a modular unit, that is a package which comes all in one and is easy to install, or a component set-up which allows you to choose as many air handlers as needed for your cabins, and to place the condenser(s), compressor(s), and water pump anywhere in the boat that's most suitable for your own situation.

Another reason expert guidance is needed in helping choose your custom air conditioner is to make optimum use of available electricity. The starting load of a high-torque motor such as used in an air con-

A *household-type air conditioner has been installed on this trawler.*

Tugboat Annie *has a recreational vehicle air conditioner.*

ditioner compressor is always far more than its running load. If you have a multi-compressor installation, an expert will see that starting loads are automatically staggered. He'll also advise you about electrolysis, which increases with the addition of each electric motor, and about the best water pump installation. Water pumps are one of marine air conditioning's chief stumbling blocks, so you need the right pump and strainer. If you need heating, an expert can incorporate the best heat source into your custom air installation.

Air conditioning aboard your boat gives you incomparable comfort in muggy weather, it helps dry the air so it comforts everyone and every*thing* in your boat, and it enhances the boat's resale value. On the minus side are cost (about $4,000 for a custom marine installation on a 35-foot power yacht), complexity with its chance of breakdowns and costs for repairs, loss of interior space that you might prefer to devote to canned goods, books, or extra fuel, and increased use of energy either through dockside power or through running your generator.

Manufacturers of marine aid conditioners include Aqua Temp, 421 N. Line St., Lansdale, PA 19446; Cummins Engine Co., 1000 Fifth St., Columbus, IN 47201; The Grunert Co., 195 Drum Pt., Osbornville, NJ 08723; Marine Air Systems, 3395 S.W. 13th Ave., Ft. Lauderdale, FL 33312; Marine Development Corp., P.O. Box 15299, Richmond, VA 23227; Sager Marine Systems, 10490 SW 186th Lane, Miami, FL 33157; Way-Wolff Associates, 45-10 Vernon Blvd., Long Island City, NY 11101.

Breezes

Not all of us can afford the price, space, and energy of mechanical air conditioning. You can do a lot with fans, both 110-volt and 12-volt models. A wide choice of both household and automatic fans, 12-volt and 110-volt, is available. If you have room to put them and power to run them, use them generously to keep the boat fresh and sweet.

Vents are also a big help in keeping air flowing through the boat. Some rely on a large horn to scoop breezes; others use a venturi effect to cram air through the boat; still others are installed over hot spots like the galley, to channel warm air away from living quarters. A concern

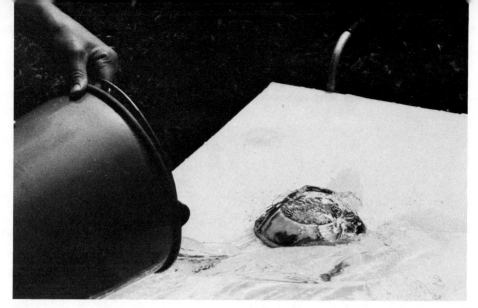

This little mushroom vent was given a water test, and passed, but leaky installations do occur.

Louvered doors on Sans Souci were well screened. These easy-to-stow stainless "storm" windows kept out too-cool breezes.

This cover fits over a wooden frame over the forepeak hatch on Sans Souci, providing standing headroom in port. Zippers open and close the flaps to admit air and keep rain out.

in any boat that will ever go to sea is that these vents don't become entryways for water. Before you hack a hole in your boat for a vent, test it. If it leaks now, it will leak later—into your *home*.

Wind Chutes

You've seen them on other boats and in boat shows, marine stores, and marine catalogues. A wind chute, also called a wind sail or a wind scoop, is a giant vent that you raise to the height and direction of the

You can easily sew your own wind catcher to channel breezes down a hatch.

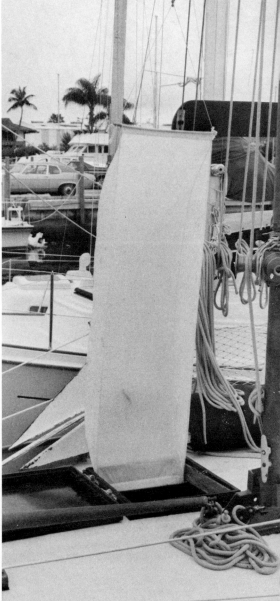

On a hot day, even an impromptu wind-catcher can cool down the boat below.

This one is easy to stow, and may funnel a welcome breeze.

A large dodger gives protection against spray from the bow. It also provides shelter from rain and cold winds at the dock.

breeze, which it then funnels into your boat. When you're at anchor, hanging into the wind, it may be enough just to raise the forward hatch to scoop the wind. It's when you're at the dock, or your boat is riding with the current rather than with the wind, that a wind scoop, which can be turned to any direction, can be most useful. Readymades are available, or you may want to design one specifically for your boat and sew it up yourself. A lightweight sail material which is tightly woven, strong, and sun resistant is a good choice and is easy for home sewing.

Features to consider in your wind chute are: (1) It should have a hold-down so it doesn't whip up out of the hatch. (2) It should be long enough to allow raising it high above the deck to catch the breeze. If, for example, you're blanked by a larger boat or by a high dock, or if low tide lowers you below breeze level, you can raise a good, long wind chute to seek out cool winds. (3) It should have some means of holding the "mouth" and "throat" open even if the winds die. This can be done with plastic hoops, a wood frame, or by tying off "arms" of the wind chute to shrouds.

Chapter 7

The Cost of Cruising

I n the early 1970's after our first year of living aboard, we wrote a story for *Yachting* about just where our money went: dockage, food, repairs, insurance, and incidentals. It amounted to about $355 per month, not counting income taxes. Although we often pointed out that there is a wide variety of tastes, appetites, boats, cruising styles, maintenance talents, and luck, we have continued to receive letters over the years asking for a pat, numerical answer to the question "What does it cost to live on board?"

Turn the question around and ask "What does it cost to live in a house?" You'd immediately answer that it depends on the size and age of the house and on how the people inside it eat, and drink, and be merry.

Some people see the dentist twice a year and others don't spend a dime on dentistry until the day they are fitted for dentures. Some boat owners maintain their vessels Bristol fashion; others merely keep a finger in the dyke; still others live for today and take their financial lumps only when something finally breaks, fails, or rots through. Some boat owners can do everything on board, from stitching sails to stitching wounds, from grinding wheat to grinding valves. Others don't know a caulking iron from a curling iron and have to hire everything out.

Costs differ because people differ. To some liveaboards, a cocktail before dinner is routine. To others it is an occasional luxury, and others never consider drinking at all. To cruise on another sailor's budget you would have to live exactly as he did, *when* he did. The international money exchange is an unknown these days. In the late 1970's, families who carried their cruising monies in Swiss Francs or Krugerands fared far better than those who were forced to barter with ever-shrinking dollars around the world. Then the dollar swelled again while the franc and the mark dwindled.

There is no easy way to compute the cost of cruising, but in answer to continuing requests we'll help you to make an educated guess. There isn't an easy way, so get out the pencil and paper.

First, make a complete list of where your money goes right now: food, housing, insurance, time payments, child support, clothing costs averaged over a year, medical and dental costs averaged over two or three years, transportation, entertainment, postage, savings, church and charity, cleaning supplies, and vacations.

See? We said it wouldn't be easy. To make such a list as complete as possible you'll probably have to go back through old check stubs and receipts, back over old tax records, review time payment obligations, and admit to yourself how much you've really been spending on liquor or the ponies.

You can cross out those items that won't apply when you move aboard, but don't be too quick with that blue pencil. The mortgage payments will go on if you decide to keep the house and rent it out. Although your tenants will pay the bills, you'll still have maintenance and management fees. Check with a management firm or realtor to get a dollar figure on what this service will cost. Then put aside about 10% of the rent each month for upkeep and repairs. They'll be far higher when hired out than when you did them yourself.

Some time payments may stop: the car if you sell it, the charge accounts if you can get caught up, the mortgage if you decide to sell the house. But what about the cemetary lots, boat payments, and TV and other items you will take aboard with you? Be honest!

Many expenses won't change much when you move aboard. You'll eat about the same, drink the same, buy newspapers and magazines, write to your friends, replace sheets and towels, fly home occasionally to see the family, continue tithing, and have a yen for the movies.

Some expenses can drop dramatically. If you've been dressing for a white collar job it's likely that you'll spend less when living on the boat in jeans. If you're a clothes horse, however, you can spend as much on sportswear as you do now on business wear. Make-up, junk jewelery, three-martini lunches, and fads of all sorts fade for many liveaboards but for others the spending goes on because old habits refuse to remain ashore. Our friend Howard, for instance, promised himself he'd quit smoking when he shed his pressure-cooker life and moved aboard. Then he decided that commissioning the boat was a lot of pressure, but he'd quit smoking when he finally got out cruising. The $30-a-month cost for cigarettes never changed.

You can cross out those costs that will definitely stop: commuter tickets and tolls, the telephone bill, pool maintenance, subscriptions and club dues—but keep your yacht club membership; reciprocity is invaluable.

In revising your list now, you'll find youself making painful decisions. Should you convert your group insurance policy to a high-cost individual plan, or cruise with no insurance at all? Will you keep your life insurance? Quit it? Raise it? Continue supporting that charity that has counted on your donation year after year? Run out on your child support or alimony? What about the care of aged parents? A college savings fund for your children? Those fabulous Christmases you're used to?

Now, while you're making an honest guess at the cost of living aboard, is a good time to face such decisions. Once you have moved aboard, problems become magnified, fears about illness or debt more overwhelming, regrets more unbearable, guilt over family duties more pressing.

Now add to your list those areas where you can make an educated guess. If you'll be living at a marina while continuing to work, this figure is an easy one because you can call the marina and ask. Even if you dream of anchoring out, there's always the chance that you won't like the isolation, can't do without power and water hook-ups, or can't find places where overnight anchoring is allowed. Have some budget for marinas, at least for the first year.

If you have financed the boat, you can list the payments in your cost column, and you also know the insurance price. By calling a boatyard you can get an idea of what hauling and bottom paint will cost for your boat (twice a year if the boat is wood; less if the boat is fiberglass or metal and if you are lucky enough to have no underwater problems).

Other expenses can also be gauged in advance. Check with a mail order school to learn what it will cost to educate your children (Chapter 13). Find a mail forwarding service (Chapter 11). Make a guess at the cost of calling your family or broker back home, and the cost of new eyeglasses each year, medications you take regularly, one or two big gift occasions a year (weddings, anniversaries, graduations).

By now you have a good idea of your expenses for food, clothing and linens, family obligations, and insurance—not counting inflation, which remains a question mark. If you'll be living on your investments, business, or other continuing source of income, you can also make a guess at your income taxes and any state or local taxes that apply to your boat (see below in this chapter).

In your list of costs, don't cross out transportation. As you cruise you'll want to explore inland by rental car, bus, or train. For major provisioning and filling gas bottles you'll need a cab or rental car. A couple of times, we put *Sans Souci* in storage during hurricane season, bought old cars, and drove north to see our families. Although the cars sold a couple of months later for what we'd paid for them, there were fuel and insurance costs.

If you plan to carry bikes or mopeds aboard they'll be high-maintenance items in a salt atmosphere. You'll also need one or two dinghies, with outboards, and fuel to run them. If you'll be living on at a local dock and continuing to work, of course, you'll continue to have auto expenses just as before.

In some columns, your expenses will be higher than they are now. Few countries in the world eat more cheaply than we do in North America. In the West Indies and parts of Europe, your food costs could double or triple. Living off the land and sea is overrated as a possibility because almost everything you find growing belongs to someone. One friend was fined $25 in the Bahamas for harvesting some bananas he thought were growing wild. Fishing is work, and not always successful. Even in those nations where fruits and vegetables are cheap, other basics are often very costly.

When you call long distance on a credit card or coin phone, bargain rates don't apply. So you'll pay more to keep in touch with your family, partner, or broker. If you're abroad, costs climb markedly. To Telex for a badly needed part and have it sent to you airmail can cost far more than a month's phone bill back home. To have your mail forwarded abroad costs, at this writing, 40 cents per *half* ounce.

In many categories (parts, food, clothing, incidentals) we found ourselves paying higher prices because, as strangers in town, we didn't know where to get the best deals. Nor did we have a car to shop around in. When you have to provision in small, non-chain markets near the water, food costs soar. Often marine needs weren't met in the small ports we visited, and we had to pay high postage costs to shop by mail.

Most doctors and dentists charge a premium price for your first visit, because of the time it takes to get your medical history, so yearly check-ups could cost more. So will health insurance after you leave your group plan.

Now you have an idea of which expenses will stop, which will go on about the same, and which will grow. From here on, you're flying blind because no one can know in advance what will break down, who will go up on a reef, when the sails or engine will blow out. Still, let's talk about the cost of boating besides the boat payments, dockage, insurance, and boat taxes which you have already listed.

The biggest factor here is how far you plan to go. The cruel truth is that many liveaboards spend far less time on the go than they planned to. But let's assume you plan to stay fairly active, even if only on weekends. Among those items you'll have to replace at intervals are:

Charts
New ones will be needed as you go. Include coast pilots, tide tables, cruising guides, guide books, nature guides for various areas, and foreign dictionaries. Buy these in increments in case you cruise more slowly than you'd planned.
Foul Weather Gear
Probable life is no more than five years.

Batteries

Probable life about three years. In addition to ship's batteries, include replacement battery for the masthead strobe, EPIRB, man-overboard marker, radios, and spotlights.

Fuel and Oil

The more carefully you have planned an itinerary the closer you can gauge fuel costs, but this one is primarily guesswork. Just because you have a sailboat, don't assume you'll travel free. Here is a report from a couple who have a 52-foot ketch. She sails like a dream even in light airs, and points well. Even so, while the couple covered 7,124 miles in 265 days they ran their engine 572 hours and the generator 610 hours, using 922 gallons of diesel fuel or 3.47 gallons per day. We figure they got about 7.72 miles to the gallon including the generator. Without the generator they would have gotten about 16 miles to the gallon— less than most of us get in a compact car. We find that most auxiliaries are used more than owners will admit. If you have a powerboat, gallon-per-hour needs can be easily computed in advance, but don't forget to allow for generator use.

Major Spares

Some spare parts are bought only during unexpected emergencies, but many have a set life so you can budget for them in advance. Again, there aren't any easy numbers. Sit down with all your owner's manuals and price out those things that need replacement every so-many hours or months: head kit, oil and fuel filters, gaskets and O-rings, oil, and spark plugs.

Major Replacements

Engine life and sail life depend greatly on how much you use them, how well you take care of them, and luck. When we sold our 20-year-old boat, the Atomic Four engine was in top condition and the mainsail still had plenty of shape. Both engine and sails had been meticulously husbanded. Offhand, we'd recommend socking away about 10% of replacement cost each year for sails, standing rigging, engine(s) and generator. Monies which aren't used for unexpected repairs along the way will be accumulating and earning interest as a hedge against that back-breaking day when replacements are needed right away.

Minor Spares

These are minor only in the sense that you won't have to keep them aboard if you stay in the city. The more remote your cruising area, the more oddball your equipment, and the less time you can afford to languish in some unwanted port while you wait for parts, the more important it will be for you to carry extensive spares such as engine bearings, valves, piston rings, valve guides, a piston, an injector, and all manner of ignition parts. In one year alone we met four skippers who had lost their oil suddenly, and burned out their bearings.

Minor Replacements

Paint, rope, varnish, sandpaper, waxes, bilge cleaner, solvents, brushes—the list is a mile long but you'll have a better idea of these ongoing costs after you've bought them for the first year's needs.

Purchases

No matter how complete your boat-home is when you move aboard there will be additional needs along the way. Herb Payson in his book *Blown Away*, described how his family found it essential to have a second dinghy. Although you'll also be shedding unneeded items after a few months of living aboard, you'll probably find you need an extra heater, a new fan, optional accessories for this and that, more emergency gear, or more electronics. This category is pure guesswork.

Services

If you can do everything aboard your boat, you'll have few costs in this column. Even the best mechanics, however, may not understand electronics or refrigeration; the best boatwrights need help with engine repairs; the most skilled navigators have to hire out upholstery or sail repair. The more strict your budget, the more important it is to eliminate those items which you can't maintain yourself, because boatyards charge $12 to $25 per hour. We've known all-thumbs boatmen who spent months in boatyards, spending thousands of dollars, just to do essential maintenance.

The Law and You

No matter how far we flee in boats, taxes pursue us. The liveaboard who keeps on the go, with a low profile, may not catch the attention of state and local authorities but will have to keep alert for what laws apply. For instance, any boat in Florida waters for six months becomes subject to state taxes even though the boat is documented, or licensed in another state. Many municipalities have harbor fees, limits on how long you can anchor, or total prohibitions on living aboard.

If you're planning to move to a certain spot for permanent living aboard, look into what state, county, or local taxes apply. Get the official story, then talk to some local liveaboards about the *real* situation. Not all taxes which are on the books are collected.

You may be able to escape taxes by leaving the state or city at intervals. When we lived aboard we licensed the boat in Florida, Alabama, New York, and once in Delaware—whatever state was cheapest at the time. Since we lived nowhere it wasn't dishonest to use any address that best suited our purposes. There is a lot of see-sawing, because a low-tax state will suddenly start singling out boats for a fleecing, so talk to other liveaboards and keep up-to-date on where the best deals are. We kept on the go so much that our boat was never in Florida waters for six months at a time, so we weren't subject to their personal property tax. Also, as you'll learn by gamming with other liveaboards, some states and counties are more vigilant than others when it comes to putting the arm on liveaboards. An effort to levy real estate tax on Florida liveaboards recently failed, but could be tried again there, and in other states too.

It may sound preachy, but the one way to avoid such scapegoating is to be neat, responsible, and conscientious about boating manners, bill paying, and behavior. When we first moved aboard in Florida, you could anchor almost anywhere, and marinas welcomed the liveaboard's dollar. Then gradually, liveaboards began getting a (partially deserved) reputation for indolence, anchoring out and sneaking ashore for free marina showers, trashing up a dock with dock boxes and freezers and mountains of deposit bottles, and running out on unpaid fuel bills. Many good liveaboards have been run out of town with the boat bums, and dockage fees at those marinas which still allow living aboard have soared.

Living aboard is really living, but the best things in life aren't free.

Throughout, I've been talking about the cost of cruising because the

A good lineup for the liveaboard: metered electricity, water, dock light, and fire protection.

question is asked so often. There is another method though. Take what money you have and take off until it's gone. Another is to work as you go, for as long as necessary. A third, if you have a fixed income, is to live within it by going only as far as you can afford to or staying at docks only as long as the money holds out. The question, we find, is not really what cruising costs, but "Can I hack it?" If you want to, of course you can!

Although you probably don't realize it at the time, the real cost of cruising begins when you start shopping for a liveaboard boat and the final total can't be known until the boat has been used, cruised, and sold at a profit or loss. We sold our boat, after ten years of use, for two and a half times her purchase price. This was only a fraction of the price of her replacement cost, due to inflation, and did not take into account the hundreds we had spent over the years on upkeep, additions, and replacements. As a business investment, our boat—compared to land or stocks or a home—was a bummer, especially during a period of fierce inflation. But there is no dollar value on the wisdom and joy that living aboard can bring.

This houseboat is within a 40-minute commute of Manhattan.

Off to the office in the morning.

Chapter 8

Liveaboard Case Histories

~~~~~~

DON AND SUE MOESLY

Growing up in Fort Lauderdale means growing up with boats, so Don Moesly has seldom been without one. His first was a $400 plywood, 14-foot kit boat with a 10 hp Mercury outboard which he built after serving in World War II. He married sweet Suzanne in 1954 and the couple began talking boats. By the early 1960's they bought the plug used for the mold of the SeaCraft 21, a fiberglass boat then being manufactured by Don's brother, Carl. The boat was elegantly equipped—Sue even caught a blue marlin aboard—but then an accident knocked boating out of the Moesly's lives, seemingly forever. Thanks to a caring orthopedic surgeon, Sue's injuries proved to be only a temporary setback, and the Moesly's were off to sea again.

The next boat was a spongy 40-foot Stonington sportfisherman that the Moesly's spent three years restoring. "By then we had $17,000 in *Pathfinder*," Sue remembers, "and everything we wanted—a flying bridge, autopilot, outriggers, steadying sail, harpoon pulpit, fighting chairs, live bait well with its own pump, a 12-foot dinghy. During a two-week vacation in the Bahamas we spent $35 for fuel because diesel was 17 cents a gallon then."

A family illiness beached the Moesly's again, and then a 33-foot ketch motorsailer caught their eye. *Sand Dollar* was shallow draft, had a Perkins diesel, and was lovingly built in Spain. *Pathfinder* went on the market for $25,000. Meanwhile, $19,000 went into the motorsailer, they quit their jobs (Don had his own furniture refinishing shop; Sue was a dental assistant) and the Bahamas beckoned.

Don and Sue Moesly's Costs

Expense	1976 (9 months) Fort Lauderdale to Galapagos	1977 Galapagos to New Zealand	1978 New Zealand to Madang, PNG	1979 Madang, PNG to Mauritius	1980 Mauritius to South Africa	1981 (6 months) South Africa to Fort Lauderdale
Groceries	$799.	$1482.	$1542.	$1993.	$2814.	$1276.
Liquor	461.	487.	849.	1280.	925.	750.
Postage	45.	143.	128.	200.	188.	65.
Dockage	297.	26.	15.	———	307.	151.
Fuel	137.	139.	322.	317.	353.	255.
Laundry	49.	14.	12.	32.	———	14.
Gifts	47.	41.	81.	32.	75.	8.
Customs and Duty Fees	101.	52.	127.	38.	72.	122.
Miscellaneous	736.	852.	1401.	1065.	1523.	692.
Subtotal	$2672.	$3236.	$4477.	$4957.	$6257.	$3333.
Boat Repairs	477.	18.	1026.	727.	1913.	208.
Boat Supplies	146.	746.	1121.	688.	808.	298.
Grand Total	$3295.	$4000.	$6624.	$6372.	$8978.	$3839.

It was during their six-month Bahamas cruise in *Sand Dollar* that Gordon and I first met Don and Sue. We'd caught a dolphin too big to eat, gave them half, and immediately liked Don's wry sense of humor and Sue's down-home, Ohio smile. (We're Buckeyes too.) The motorsailer took them as far as the Turks and Caicos Islands before they began thinking about living aboard and long-range cruising. The boat they chose, *Svea*, was a heavy, double-ended 38-foot ketch that had already been sailed around the world by Bob and Mary Kittredge. Don took a part-time job with a furniture refinishing shop and Sue worked in a boatyard while they prepared *Svea* for the second time around. By then they had $50,000 invested in their boat-home and her equipment. Their first year at sea, 1976, cost them $6,000, then $7,000, $8,000, $9,000, and by 1980 they spent $10,000 a year because of inflation and the weakened dollar. *Svea* has been sold now, and the Moesly's haven't yet decided on their next adventure. They don't want to circumnavigate again—ever—but the sea will always be a part of their lives and the Bahamas remain their favorite cruising grounds.

There are pages more to this story, but I don't have to tell it because Sue has already written her own book. Watch for it to come on the market.

KATHI AND CHARLIE HAST

By the early 1970's, with five children aged three through 11, the Hasts were beginning to worry about California's drug scene, and about lifestyles they found shallow. This wasn't where they wanted their children to live their teen years, but an alternative didn't occur to them until their first sail. And they were smitten. "Not only did it seem to be the perfect way to relax, it would offer an opportunity for the entire family to experience other cultures," Kathi says now.

The whole Hast clan began building *Sunday Morning* in September of 1970, launched her in Febraury of 1973, and moved aboard the following June. While building the boat, the Hasts also took every available Power Squadron class, and practiced sailing a 14-foot dinghy in Newport Harbor. After another three years of weekend sailing while living aboard at marinas, the family was ready to try its wings. On February 29, 1976, they left the dock for the Marquesas, went on to sail the southern Pacific, Polynesia, New Zealand, the New Hebrides, the Solomons, New Guinea, south to Australia, across the Indian Ocean, down the coast of South Atlantic to Brazil and up through the Caribbean. They hit home shores again on the 4th of July, 1981.

How did two adults and five children survive? After selling their home and businesses in California, they invested the monies and harvested an income of $500 month, which Kathi says was more than enough in 1976. Hauling, repairs, reprovisioning—everything was covered for $6,000 a year. By the second year they were down to three children on the boat, there wasn't extra money for rental cars, restaurants and other luxuries.

"Still, we were traveling first class," Kathi beams. *Sunday Morning* is a 67-foot LOA ferro-cement schooner, roomy and comfortable on long passages. Although they chose not to continue repairing and re-repairing refrigeration and freezer systems, they have five 20-pound propane tanks and never worry about running short of stove fuel. Kathi carries whole wheat, which she grinds fresh for bread after finding that flour didn't keep well in the steamy Pacific. She cans meat, fish, fruits, and vegetables, and also dries fish, meat, and fruits.

After the family settled down temporarily in Stuart, Florida, the children slipped right into the high school curriculum and started bringing home A's and B's, unharmed by their five years of mail order schooling. "Cruising kids become avid readers, and our World Book Encyclopedia was well read, and so was every paperback available," Charlie says.

"As soon as the two youngest children are out of high school, we'll be off again," vows Charlie, who has gone back to work for the duration. "We figure now it would cost us about $900 a month to cruise internationally." A few weeks later Kathi wrote again with the news that she too had found a job, the teenagers were learning to drive, and all the family were enjoying the luxuries of land living: bicycles, new clothes, Pac-Man, ice cream, and the "release from the constant vigilance needed when sailing." Kathi believes now that $1,000 to $1,200 per month will be needed to cruise comfortably.

AL AND BETH LIGGETT

On their first date, Al and Beth went sailing aboard Al's 20-foot sloop, and it was love at first sight: he, she, and the boat. They went out evenings and weekends on the sloop in Newport Beach, looked out on the big sailboats with a hint of Catalina showing through the smog, and their dream of long-distance sailing began.

They bought *Bacchus* in 1965 in Annapolis and left her in storage there while they went back to California to study navigation and sell their "unnecessaries" as Beth dubs them. The boat was a 40-foot flush deck ketch, very heavy with a long keel and seven-foot draft. She took the couple around the world in four years. Returning to California in 1970, they sold *Bacchus* and started on another grubstake for another circumnavigation.

Two years later they moved to Guam, looking for financial opportunities and a nice place to live. While there they commissioned Robert Perry to do a custom design, which was executed in Airex foam core at a small yard in Taiwan. *Sunflower* was launched in 1976. She's a 42-foot cutter, flush deck, easy to handle, and comfortable for living aboard. In the next few years, the Liggetts sailed more than 33,000 miles to the Philippines, Japan, Solomons, Papua New Guinea, Indonesia, Singapore, Borneo, back to the Phillippines, Hong Kong, Japan again, then across the North Pacific to Victoria, B.C. In the summer of 1981 they cruised Canada and Southeastern Alaska.

Aboard their first boat they were able to get by on about $2,500-$3,000 a year, but costs have been rising steadily from $6,000 in 1977, $6,500, $8,000, then in 1980 they spent $9,700 which included some big medical expenses, an engine overhaul and three new sails. For their five months of cruising in 1981 the total was $2,500, but this does not reflect pre-cruising and post-cruising costs, which were always, for us, the primary expenses of the year.

CAROLE AND DON HOROWITZ

It all began in San Francisco where Don, a lifelong boating enthusiast, had a 32-foot yawl. For the sake of their relationship Carole, who had never been aboard anything larger than a rowboat, really tried to like sailing in cold, rough, wet San Francisco Bay but it wasn't until they moved to Texas and had the boat shipped to Galveston that she discovered the joy of sailing in sheltered waters. Now, although she had no intention of ever making a home afloat with Don and their four children from previous marriages, she began to know and like sailing.

When Don saw an ad for a 40-year-old, 65-foot motorsailer in Florida at a price they couldn't resist, they plunged—sight unseen. With great plans they set off for Florida to bring the boat to Texas to restore her, but the sail was a fiasco. Undaunted, they sold everything in the house, packed up the three children who now lived with them, and moved to Florida to resurrect the boat of their dreams.

"Something had happened meanwhile that made us see we could manage on a boat, despite the hardships of living aboard while doing the restoration," Carole remembers now. "When we first arrived in Texas, our home wasn't ready so we had to put our things in storage and camped out in a semi-furnished apartment. We made it fun to eat from paper plates and plastic forks, use a cheap drop cloth for a shower curtain, and cut our meat by passing around our one bayonet knife. We realized that we didn't really miss all the junk that was in storage, except for our books and records. Moving to our boat would not be that big a change."

By the time they got to the boat, however, she was mildewed and stinking after four months in the Florida sun. Carole wanted to go home, but this *was* home. The children adapted like troopers, started school at Daytona, and the family set up housekeeping in a marina. "For the next few years we worked like demons and lived like paupers," Carole says now, "but in retrospect it was one of the best times we ever had. We managed to sail to the Bahamas for a three-week vacation."

Finally the boat was in Bristol condition and ready for sale. The boat was taken to Fort Lauderdale, two of the children moved to California to live with other parents, and one stayed with Carole and Don. But selling was easier said than done. Carole took a job as a window trimmer in a dress shop to keep the wolf from the door, while Don stayed with the boat, keeping her in spiffy condition for a buyer who didn't show up until nine agonizing, frustrating months later. Within a few months they found a 33-foot Swedish sloop which they lived aboard for six years—cruising six months at a time when they could.

∞∞∞∞∞∞∞∞∞∞∞∞∞∞∞∞∞∞∞∞∞∞∞∞∞∞∞∞∞∞∞∞∞∞∞∞∞∞∞

After living at a dock in east-central Florida where both Carole and Don had jobs, Carole said, "Living on a boat while cruising is fine, but as a floating apartment when you are working, our boat was too small. Something in the 40- 50-foot range would be ideal, a shower is a must, and an oven would be wonderful. I never minded the inconveniences, but I would have loved more luxuries such as hot water.

"Living aboard is cheaper than living ashore, but it can be just as expensive if you have a phone, two cars, etc. We had two old cars and no phone, and were lucky to have very cheap dock rent. Anchoring out is cheaper still, but it's not practical for a working couple. After eight years of living aboard, I was tired of it. I wanted a small house or apartment, a dishwasher, a bathtub. If we had the money to keep cruising, it would be different, but two years of living aboard and working and going nowhere is boring. So much accumulated, we finally rented a storage locker ashore—always a no-no for us before.

"Cruising is an inexpensive way to live aboard, but we can no longer live on $25 worth of food a week as we did when we first moved aboard. When we first went to the Bahamas, it cost $100 a month while there and $800 to buy six months of food before we went. Our other expenses included $500 a year for insurance, and food for our Doberman who is our early warning device."

In the spring of 1982, after living at the dock and working ashore for two years in Melbourne, Florida, Don found a management job in Huntsville and the couple have moved there to the kind of apartment Carole wanted during the two years of dockside living. *Caradon* remains at her dock in Florida, closed up and waiting for their return. And return they promise to do because they still feel that cruising is the best life of all!

SKIP AND LINDA DASHEW

If the name looks familiar it's because Skip's articles appear often in boating magazines, and the couple authored *Circumnavigator's Handbook* (W.W. Norton). Before their liveaboard days, Skip gained fame racing small catamarans. Linda, who grew up in Idaho and was teaching in Salt Lake City, started flying to Los Angeles for weekend regattas, teamed up with Skip, and won the Shark class national championships in 1966. *Beowulf* V, their D class catamaran, set the world record for speed under sail in 1971, by averaging 35.58 miles an hour. They went on in class cats, and won five more world championships.

By 1972 the couple had two baby girls and wanted to include them in the sailing, so they fitted out a new 37-foot cat with two bunks, a stove, and a portable potty. On short races, they removed the house and sailed with the trampoline only. On her first race, *Beowulf* VI walked away with all the roses—first to finish and first on corrected time. Skip raced her to Ensenada, and Linda cruised home with him after adding the boat's camping gear. It was such fun, they started thinking seriously about big-boat cruising.

Then one day Skip, flying home on a business trip, picked up a magazine and read about other people who were changing their lifestyles in mid-career, and he arrived home full of arguments—which weren't needed because Linda agreed to go sailing.

Intermezzo was a Bill Tripp design, custom built by Columbia. She was a 50-footer drawing 7 feet, 12 feet abeam, and with a 36-foot waterline. She had been built for racing, yet the robust hull showed no sign of stress, so the Dashews knew this was a boat that could stand the gaff. They changed the yawl rig to ketch, modified the interior for cruising, added a double bunk to make a master stateroom forward, and put a pantry in one head. By the time they reached New Zealand, they added an aft cabin.

When they left California in November of 1976, they planned to cruise French Polynesia and Hawaii for about nine months, using the time to think through their priorities of life. By now Skip's business, supplying forms to contractors who were building high-rise concrete buildings, was more headache than pleasure to him. They sold out, and sailed around the world.

"Expenses were less than we would have thought," Linda reports. "Once we bought the boat, our yearly costs averaged $8,000 for everything including hiring cars for sightseeing, eating out at nice restaurants, updating our wardrobes, repairs and diesel for the boat. Everything. There were very few places that charged harbor fees, and we avoided busy ports in favor of quieter, more isolated anchorages. Of course, cruising would cost far more if one used marinas on a regular basis."

During the first 3 1/2-year cruise they sailed the South Pacific, crossed the Tasman to New Zealand, went to New Caledonia, New Hebrides, Solomons, and New Guinea. They sailed the Indian Ocean going from Australia to Bali, Christmas Island, Cocos Keeling, Rodrigous, Mauritius, South Africa, and then across the Atlantic from Cape Town to the Virgin Islands and on to Fort Lauderdale. Their new boat, *Intermezzo II* is a 62-foot aluminum cutter displacing 49,700 pounds.

When I last heard from the Dashews they were living in Fort Lauderdale, but they find that it's getting more and more difficult to live aboard there. Most canals are zoned for single family dwelling, which makes it illegal for liveaboards to rent in such areas. At Hendricks Isle and Isle of Venice, boat slips rent for about $350 a month. Pier 66 and Bahia Mar were charging 75 cents/foot/day in 1982 and Linda found one marina charging 35 cents/foot/day. "We know one home owner willing to rent dock space for $500 a month plus electricity and water," Linda reports. "It's not cheap living."

MARGUERITE AND IAN WATSON

Although the others who shared case histories with us were sailors, hundreds more liveaboards have powerboats of all styles and sizes. The Watsons, who are originally South African, not only lived cozily aboard their 36-foot, aft cabin, British-design *Moonraker*, they cruised the Bahamas extensively with their baby boy.

The boat, Marguerite reports, has an aft cabin with one double and one single bunk, an enclosed wheelhouse, then head, galley, and vee berth forward. As time neared for the baby to be born, Marguerite made bunk sheets for the single by cutting a bed sheet in half, made a padded lee board, and made more cushions by covering pads she took out of an old flotation cushion. By the time baby Bevan appeared in March of 1979, he had a cozy and safe bunk for all sea conditions.

When the baby was three months old, he was moved forward to the port vee berth. Marguerite nursed the baby for ten months, made all her own baby food aboard, and relied on disposable diapers which required, she remembers, "many trips to the garbage hopper, 20 yards down the dock." She found her front baby carrier was ideal for holding the baby safely, freeing both her hands while she got off and on the boat. The chief problem was laundromats. When the baby was fussy it was an unhappy time for both mother and son, and when he began crawling he was into everything.

By the time Bevan was five months old, Marguerite decided that a lee board wasn't enough protection, so she made a playpen-crib out of real fish net, nylon line, and hooks. Swimming lessons for the baby began at two months, and at six months he could swim underwater. Now, at age three, he still gets swimming lessons and loves the water.

Although they kept a high board in the companionway so Bevan couldn't wander out of the wheelhouse, they also bought a child harness which they modified with a new, stronger line. Underway, the toddler was always attached to a sturdy hook somewhere anytime Mom was forward and busy with lines and Pop was at the wheel. Bevan wore a Kindergaard infants' vest when they went into the dinghy, for the crossing to the Bahamas, and while swimming. When the boy was 16 months old, the family moved ashore but kept the boat, which is docked in a canal behind the house.

By age two and a half, Bevan graduated from his inflatable arm bands to flippers and freestyle, still swimming with his head underwater. The couple plan to stay actively in boating, probably with a sailboat of about 30 feet.

FRANK AND IRIS JONES

They've owned five boats but it wasn't until Frank retired as a TWA captain in 1969 that they sold their home and 21 acres, airplane, horses, and the "whole works" in an auction that they still recall as "traumatic" and moved aboard. Since then they've cruised more than 30,000 miles, sideswiped three hurricanes, taken the brunt of Hurricane Allen which did $10,000 in damage to their boat, and bashed through more Gulf cold fronts than they want to remember. Their roomy, comfortable 1953 Chris Craft Constellation is powered by two GMC 671's and is 58 feet overall.

After finding the liveaboard climate in Florida increasingly hostile (dock fees have soared; so have the numbers of communities that ban living aboard), they've finally settled on Texas as a home base but they cruise back to Florida on visits.

Iris, an Oklahoma girl who never learned how to lasso until she had to put a line around a bollard, likes living aboard better than mowing 21 acres of grass and weathering icy winters. She misses a bathtub, washer and dryer, but does have a microwave oven, stereo throughout the boat, wet bar, plenty of refrigerator and freezer space, and an electric organ. Among her treasures she also lists "sunny skies, blue-green waters, fascinating shells on sand beaches, and quaint towns."

Living aboard, Frank reports, costs them about $1,500 a month. They'll be celebrating a golden wedding aboard in 1985.

JUDY AND LEON CRITZ

Judy's allergies were so widespread and severe that she spent several weeks each year in the hospital with asthma. Then the family began to realize that her symptoms weren't as bad when they were aboard their 36-foot houseboat, and the doctor suggested living aboard. Life aboard for Judy and Leon, and the two boys, ages 11 and 16, who still lived at home, was so successful that Judy was able to work fulltime. They sold their home, bought a 40-foot houseboat, and two years later ordered their 43-foot Carlcraft fiberglass, vee-hull houseboat. It has a flybridge, bathtub, and two complete bedrooms. "It was worth waiting for," says Judy who headquarters at Las Vegas Boat Harbor, "and we have traveled the entire 500-mile shoreline of Lake Mead.

The houseboat cost $40,000, which was about the same as they would have paid for a home in the late 1970's. They pay $416 a month on the boat plus $193 a month dockage which includes 30-amp electrical service, water, covered slip, and night watchman. Other expenses include commuting, and $600 a year for insurance. They've survived three major storms with winds up to 110 knots and still wouldn't go back to the land living. After the boys are gone the plan to cruise more widely, perhaps with a trawler.

What advice does Judy Critz have for the future liveaboard? "Space is essential and you won't be able to have all the things you have in a house. Everyone must compromise. Every month we all go through and take things off the boat or the waterline would go down, down, down. Also, we have to plan our shopping more closely because it's a long trip into town. And, if you're still a working couple, you need lots of closet space because you have to dress well."

With the roominess of a houseboat the Critz's are able to have some comforts that won't fit into smaller boats. One of theirs is an electric organ which, they report, gives them no electronic problems.

"You have to adapt or go back ashore. Most of our friends who have moved aboard have done it in stages, a week at a time, then a month. They they sell the house and make the big step."

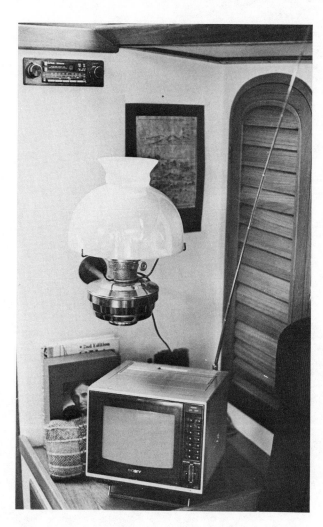

A small TV, *a car stereo, a favorite print, and an electrified gimbaled lamp— none takes up much space, but each helps make a boat a home.*

PART TWO

THE LIVEABOARD LIFE

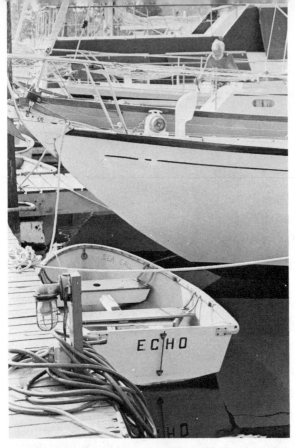

A sailing tender, labeled with her own name and her mothership's name, waits under the bow.

There are many choices to be made regarding a suitable tender: motor? stability and carrying capacity? portability?

Chapter 9

Fitting It All In

~~~~~~

A list of all the things to be stowed in a liveaboard boat versus a weekend or vacation boat sounds like a household inventory. The Christmas decorations, income tax records going back several years, out-of-season clothes, the sewing machine, books and tapes. You need not only everyday galley equipment, but extras for company, and perhaps canning and preserving supplies. Not only clothes and linens for a week or two, but plenty of spares for those times when you're on short water rations or can't get to the laundry. Food for weeks, perhaps months. Tools, spares, hobby equipment, cameras, and typewriter.

Stowage problems begin in the showroom, when you see that spacious cabin with all its bins and cubbyholes. Before you buy the boat, take a close inventory of how much stowage space is really available. Under-bunk stowage may already be filled with water tanks; lockers may already be half-filled with plumbing, pumps, ducts, and other space-stealers.

The two stowage problems most overlooked by liveaboards until too late are sails and the dinghy. If the sails are aboard the showroom boat at all, they're in the hanging locker—which you'll need for clothes. Some, of course, will be on the deck at all times, but where will you keep those bulky, extra sails?

The Dinghy

If you'll be living dockside, it won't be a major consideration, but for cruising sailors the dinghy—which often is added as an afterthought—becomes the most important boating accessory of all. 129

It's your ticket to shopping and all other shoreside delights, it helps you set anchors, it takes you fishing or visiting, it lets you sound tricky coves before you venture in with the big boat, it's your work platform for painting and cleaning the topsides, and it may also be a lifeboat. We bought a special gas cylinder for our Avon Redcrest dinghy, so it could be partially inflated in seconds in an emergency. If there are two or more people aboard, with different jobs or interest, you may even need two dinghies just as modern families have two cars.

Our first tender was a fiberglass pram, and we were warned that we'd lose it eventually if we towed it. Yet we simply had no room aboard little *Sans Souci* to stow a dinghy on deck, and no room for davits either. Sure enough, we lost it at sea two years later, towing it through a violent northerly. By then, inflatables were in widespread distribution, so we replaced it with the Avon.

There are lots of dinghy choices to be made: inflatable or rigid, powered or oared or sail, size, quality, whether to carry it in davits, or on deck, or towed astern. We still have our Avon, and have always found it to be a sturdy, durable, convenient, unsinkable workhorse. Folded properly, it can be secured on deck in a space the size of two fat bed pillows. It is an ideal boat to swim from, easy to board from the water—unlike our rigid dinghy, which upset. It also rides nicely alongside the boat, without scarring or bumping as hard dinghies can. Powered by our Johnson 3 hp outboard, the Avon is slow but economical and dependable.

However, and I think this would go for most inflatables: it takes time to inflate the boat and even longer to clean and deflate it properly. Yet it has to be done every time you get underway, or you're back in the towing trap again. Also your inflatable will last longer if you keep it clean and out of the sun. Inflatables are beasts to row in the best conditions, and are real sloths in any wind. Unless you add floorboards they're difficult to move around in, and there are usually puddles where you want to put the grocery bags. Yet floorboards add weight and take up space in your boat.

The dinghy is an important a piece of liveaboard equipment as your car is on shore. Choose yours, and its carrying method, with care, and it will not become a hindrance.

~~~~~~

His, Hers, and Ours

Although *Sans Souci* was small compared to most of the other liveaboard boats we met over the years, Gordon and I never fought about space. It's important that everyone aboard have stowage areas that are his alone, without someone questioning why you need all that junk or what are you going to do with THAT for crying out loud. You'll have to work out your own system, but generally everything abaft the companionway was his for tools, snorkel gear, spares, sails, and extra anchors. Without disturbing me in the galley, he could do almost any maintenance or repair job on the boat or load all the gear into the dinghy for a fishing, diving, shopping, or picnic expedition.

My turf was the galley and most of the other areas below. My typewriter and writing files were kept behind the starboard seat; charts and Gordon's cameras were kept to port. Books, tapes, and hanging locker were "ours" and we each had hammocks in the forepeak for our own clothes and current reading material. I never kicked about how many old copies of *Road and Track* he kept on board as long as they fit into his magazine rack, and he never questioned why a woman living in the middle of nowhere needs four kinds of perfume and eleven shades of lipstick.

When Christmas came, weeks away from our last shopping port, both of us were able to pull out a few surprises for the other. That's another of the reasons to have a few spots, no matter how small, which are completely and privately your own.

Divide and Conquer

When you see a huge, gaping, under-bunk stowage bin in the showroom it looks like Mammoth Cave. But one of the most annoying things about life aboard is that every time you want something, it's under three or four other things. We found it best to use removable compartments for such big bins, rather than trying to fit them with permanent sections. Unused bunks and quarter berths are also spacious stowage areas, once you can divide and utilize the cubic footage.

Dishpans make excellent dividers. Our entire hand towel supply fit into one; the dish towels in another. The first-aid kit fit into a plastic shoe box. Big, plastic "milk" cartons hold a case of canned goods, and can be shifted around as needed. Eddie Bauer, P.O. Box 3700, Seattle, WA 98124, carries one that knocks down flat, which makes it ideal for temporary use such as a laundry basket.

The Bauer catalogue also lists heavy net bags, which are good for corralling oddsize items such as sweaters, fruits and vegetables, frozen food, and snorkel gear. For smaller items such as folding hats, sweaters, and windbreakers, I use ribknit tops cut from worn-out socks. Each item can be rolled, slipped into this tube, and stowed neatly in a small space. The sock tops can also be drawn over canning jars and liquor bottles to keep them from breaking.

The more dividing and subdividing you can do, the easier it is to find what you want when you're rummaging in a hammock, duffel bag, or deep, dark locker. One small bag can hold lipsticks, another the cookie cutters, another your supply of ball point pens, another small bits of line. Into one large box, put small jars (baby food jars are ideal) containing screws and bolts. If you don't have space for a spice rack on a bulkhead, keep spice bottles together in one box which can be removed all at once from a galley locker.

Although we each had a plastic dishpan for personal items such as toothbrush, shaver, and cosmetics, it's also useful to have a doff kit for each person aboard for times when you want to use shoreside showers. I made simple bags out of poplin, with a couple of extra pockets on the side, and sturdy poplin handles. Today as we travel aboard many boats of all types, these bags are still indispensable. There is room in them for personal needs when you go into the common head to shave or shower but, if you go ashore for showers, the bags are roomy enough to carry basics such as soap box and deodorant plus a towel and fresh clothing. Don't forget the handles. About half the shower stalls I go into have no room for clothes, towels, and other shower equipment. Yet there's usually a hook, nail, or a doorknob where my bag can hang, clean and dry.

Classified Stowage

We all have to work out our own system based on what we carry and how much room we have to carry it in. Aboard *Sans Souci* we had ready stowage areas where I kept everyday galley supplies such as flour, sugar, spices, coffee, and other things that were used daily. We could easily raise the cabin sole to get at other stowage areas where I kept canned meat in one section, vegetables in another, fruits in a third, and miscellaneous items such as soups and condiments in another. Paper products, which are lighter in weight, were kept as high as possible in the boat and heavier items low, in our dry bilge.

In addition to the ready stowage, and the handy areas where more canned goods were kept, we had areas which we called dead stowage (under bunks, behind drawers), and others which were called dead-dead because it required major dismantling to get into them. Our lazarette and cockpit lockers, for instance, were cavernous but had a floor. By removing everything from the lockers, then taking out the floorboards, we could find room for an extra anchor with a couple of hundred feet of line, a case of toilet paper, half a case of paper towels, and a couple of cubic feet of miscellaneous supplies.

Ready stores were mixed items, things I reached for every day. Nearby were the bins where I could reach fairly easily for canned this or that. Less handy stowage areas were filled with a variety of items so, by emptying them, I could replenish each of the ready lockers. After we'd been out for several months, and finally were forced to delve into dead-dead, we found there a good supply of canned goods of all types, coffee, flour, paper goods, and other needs to resupply all the ready lockers. Other dead-dead areas were saved for holiday decorations, business records that had to be saved, and luggage needed only once or twice a year.

If you'll be cruising from one foreign port to another, you'll also need a lockable locker for bonded stores. This allows you to buy duty-free items (spell that l-i-q-u-o-r), which must be locked up until you leave that port.

One of my most useful, temporary stowage bins was the inelegant paper grocery bag, made sturdier by putting one inside the other. Each time we left Florida for the Bahamas, we had large supplies of items which would be gone very quickly—too quickly to merit squirreling them away carefully. Loaves of "store" bread, fresh fruit, and bulky boxed cookies and snacks were a luxury for the week or two it took us to get to the southern Bahamas. In paper bags, I also kept a supply of

This library is ready to go to sea in its own locker. Liveaboards, young and old, seem to do a lot of reading on board.

Here are bottles wrapped for protection, candle holders tucked away for later use, and a stereo speaker mounted inside the louvered door.

In this boat the fo'c's'le is for guests, and for off-season clothes' storage.

Old socks can become useful in cushioning bottles and jars.

quick foods which were easy to reach and prepare in rough seas. When these quickly consumed foods were gone, I folded the paper bags and put them away, while my other lockers remained filled.

Stow It and Secure It

There's nothing more disconcerting to the new liveaboard than to have a neat, smoothly running, floating household that comes completely unglued the first time a little wake nudges the boat. Even well-stowed supplies can come loose in big seas, and I've known people who lived aboard the same boat for years without trouble until the day the Ultimate Wave pried loose things that had never budged before.

The first step is to appreciate the monstrous forces at work. In even a slight heel canned goods shift against a locker door, and can break through unless the lock is a good one. Unless you'll be in only the tamest waters, trailer-style door and drawer latches just won't do the job. Many of them these days are made of plastic, and don't even hold up in the trailers. A sturdy wood toggle, by contrast, is cheap and easy to make, easy to lock and unlock, and strong.

Countertop items (microwave, toaster oven) if you have them should be screwed down. Book shelves need wood slat supports across the front. Shock cord isn't enough to hold heavy items in high seas. Neither is florist's clay, although it is a popular stick-down for small, decorative, shelf items.

The dinghy, if it's carried right side up, should have a sturdy cover with a ridge pole to shed water. Otherwise a rogue wave can fill it suddenly with water, tripling its weight and jerking it loose from its lashings. Carried upside down, the dinghy should be held down with sturdy line secured to well-set fastenings.

Finding space for all your life's impedimenta is half the battle. The rest is in keeping it from coming unstowed when the going gets tough.

Chapter 10

Cash Flow on the Go

It was a kind of culture shock. I was accustomed to driving up to the bank window, handing over a check, and getting in return a deposit slip, some cash, and a cheerful hello. All that changed when we arrived in Fort Lauderdale, where everyone behaved as though we had come to carry off a big Brinks job. The cashier's check we'd bought to bankroll our fitting-out was refused by the bank, and so were our travelers checks, at a discount store. In time we learned to deal with both the problems of paying bills when you're always a stranger in town, and with the feeling of being non-persons who are greeted with suspicion, if not downright scorn.

One of our favorite ways of carrying safe and available cash in the States is U.S. Savings Bonds, because they continue to draw interest until you cash them in. One copy of the serial numbers is kept with you and another is sent to a relative, so you're protected if the bonds are lost or stolen. Not only are they free, where many brands of travelers checks are not (American Express travelers checks cost $1 per $100), they are also as easy or easier to cash.

When we encountered a Fort Lauderdale banker who balked at our bonds, we wrote the Treasury Department asking why bankers who are allowed to sell the bonds are not also required to redeem them. The letter we received has been carried with us ever since. Any institution which sells bonds is required to redeem them in "reasonable" amounts when presented "reasonable" identification. We renewed our passport to use as identification. And we redeem only $100 in bonds at one time. If you are refused, report the banker to the Feds.

⚡⚡⚡⚡⚡⚡⚡⚡⚡⚡⚡⚡⚡⚡⚡⚡⚡⚡⚡⚡⚡⚡⚡⚡⚡⚡⚡

There are some bad points to using bonds. One is that they pay pitiable interest compared to other savings instruments. At this writing, Series EE bonds are paying 9%. We use them only for traveling cash. (If your income will suddenly drop or stop when you move aboard, however, savings bonds look more attractive because you pay tax on the interest during the year you *collect* it.) The other drawback is that they must be held for at least six months before they can be cashed. So start buying them before you start your cruise. Also, they can be redeemed only in the United States. They can't be cashed abroad, not even in foreign branches of American banks.

Despite the initial cost of travelers checks, and the fact that you earn no interest on money tied up in them, they have some advantages over bonds. They are usually accepted by individuals, marinas, bars, restaurants, and retail stores. Bonds can be redeemed only at banks or savings and loans, during banking hours. You can usually find somebody to cash a travelers check at any hour of the day or night, Sundays and holidays. We often have a few on hand, in smaller denominations, which are more readily accepted by small businesses.

To balance the rebuffs we've had there have been many kindnesses, usually in smaller towns where peoples' instinct is to like and trust others. In dealing with banks, we always find that it's best to level with them about our situation. "We're strangers here so we don't expect instant cash," we explain, "but we're not in any hurry so we'd appreciate your telling us how we can best send in this check for collection." The longest it has taken has been a week, but some banks made transfers for us after confirming by telephone. You never know, so don't let your cash reserves get too low.

By using checks as much as possible, we cut down on the amounts of cash we have to keep on hand. We always try checks first and they are always accepted for services from doctors and boat yards, for the amount of a purchase in smaller stores or marinas, and—once in a blue moon—for cash. And checks are used for paying bills by mail. Social Security and other income checks can be deposited directly in your checking account and you may be able to arrange some other automatic deposit, through your broker or through a savings account in the same bank. Anything that bypasses the complicated mail problems suffered by liveaboards is desirable (see the chapter on Mail Call).

When you move aboard, unless you'll be staying on in your home town, shop around for the best deal on a checking account. If you'll be doing much of your banking by mail anyway, it doesn't matter whether you bank in Alaska or Arkansas. Some checking accounts pay interest if you maintain a minimum balance, which varies from bank to bank. Some checking accounts are non-interest-paying but are free and have no minimum balance. Some are free if you have another account with the same bank.

Money management accounts, handled by stockbrokers, pay high interest rates and have free check-writing features. Every day of "float," which is the time between when your check is written and when it is presented for payment, is money in your pocket because of these high interest rates. The one drawback to these accounts is that you need a hefty initial investment, usually $10-$20,000. One such account is Merrill Lynch's Cash Management Account, which has several nice features including checks, and access to your funds via your Visa Card at any participating bank. Dean Witter Reynolds has a choice of money-management plans with check-writing privileges. So does your broker.

While your checking and savings accounts can continue by mail from where you are to whatever financial institution suits your needs, a safety deposit box—if you want one—can't be moved around electronically the way funds can be. If you want a trusted relative or friend to have access to the box while you're out cruising, fill out the necessary forms at the bank.

There are two special warnings. One is that, in some states, a safety deposit box is sealed if one party dies. Even though everything in the box belongs to you, it could be tied up for months in such states if your other signatory dies. The second problem for the liveaboard is that most banks do not insure the contents of safe-deposit boxes. In the unlikely event that yours are stolen, they are covered by a home owner's policy—which you, as a liveaboard, no longer have. Talk to your bank and to your insurance broker to see if a special policy is available. Before you give up your home owner's insurance, by the way, look into other coverage you've always taken for granted (such as a clause covering you if your golf ball slugs another player or insuring your baggage if it is lost while you're on vacation). The policy for your boat-home will be far different, and you may need extra policies.

Charge cards can be a mixed blessing. Even if you're accustomed to paying bills on time, you may end up paying a lot in interest because of mail delays. Still, we find they are cheap insurance against finding ourselves broke in a town where we can't cash checks. It costs about $30 a year for the prestige cards; about half that for bank cards. We have one bank card, several fuel credit cards, and charge cards for Sears and Penney's.

One of the most useful credit cards is from the telephone company. As liveaboards we used pay phones (or sometimes the telephones of friends or businesses) for ten years. Without the charge card we would always have been scrambling for enough coins, or putting calls on friends' bills. If you can get a credit card before you give up your home phone, do so. Applying for the card when you have no telephone number is almost comic. If that's the case don't even bother talking to regular telephone service personnel. They haven't the foggiest idea how to deal with the special problem you present them. Get right through to a supervisor and, if you get no results, ask to talk to his/her supervisor. We insisted that we had a flawless record with the Bell System, and so did my parents, whose address we used. Eventually someone talked sense, and we've had the credit card ever since.

Using a telephone credit card, you'll never qualify for rock-bottom rates, but you can save by calling evenings and weekends. As more and more phone companies do away with the old service of allowing callers to charge a call to a third number, the credit card becomes increasingly valuable. The surcharge for credit calls is the same as that for collect and other operator-assisted calls. U.S. telephone credit cards are accepted in some, but not all, other countries.

Charge cards carry one subtle benefit that many people don't know about. The merchant can give you the discount in cash. Here's how it works. When you charge a purchase or a meal, the businessman pays a percentage to the card company. For bank cards it's about 4%; the prestige cards may charge him as much as 10%. As long as he's out a percentage anyway when you charge the item, he may elect to give you this discount for paying cash. That way he gets his money now instead of later. It doesn't work in large stores where you're dealing with employees who never heard of this policy, but we have used it in smaller restaurants and stores where we're dealing with the owners. We've also been able to work it with fuel cards. In fact, some marinas charge one price for cash sales and another for charges.

Charge cards can also be used to get cash. The policy varies from company to company, account to account, so check with your own charge company to find out what you qualify for. Go to a bank which deals in Visa or Mastercard, get a cash advance on your account just as if you were charging dinner or a new hat, and they'll phone for confirmation just as any other merchant does. It's quick and easy money in the U.S. (it is not available at all banks abroad, even those which have other Visa/Mastercard services) but the interest rate is high. At this writing, it's about 18% depending on the state. You pay from the day of withdrawal to the day you pay the bill, unlike other purchases on which you pay interest only if you're late in paying the monthly bill. There may also be a state stamp tax on the funds. In Florida it is 15 cents per $100.

Another way to get quick cash is to have it wired to you. A friend or relative takes the cash to a Western Union office, and gives them your name and information on how to reach you when it arrives. The cost varies according to how much is sent, but $500 can be wired within the U.S. for less than $25. To Europe it's about twice that amount. The money arrives in hours, depending on how busy the wires are.

The U.S. mails are a quick, inexpensive way to transfer money and you'll probably be able to cash a postal money order more easily than a check. Although not all post offices carry international Money Orders, you can get domestic M.O.s anywhere. For a $50 to $500 M.O. you pay only $1.55, and it's cashed for you at the post office. (It's unlikely, however, that a small post office will have as much as $500 on hand.) If you're in a real hurry for the money, have the M.O. sent via Express Mail.

Express Mail is not available between all post offices, and the rules can be confusing because there are two services. One is post office to post office, costing a minimum of $5.85 depending on weight and distance. Your back-home friend mails the check at the post office before the deadline, and you must pick up your Express letter the following day, any time after 10 a.m. If it doesn't arrive as promised, the postage is refunded. Express mail can also be sent to your marina address. That costs about $9.35 for any packet up to two pounds. It's important that you confirm with your post office that Express Mail is available at both the sending and receiving points (small post offices don't have it), and whether you're getting home or post office delivery. We once paced the decks for days waiting an Express Mail letter that was waiting for us at the post office.

Cash and other negotiable wealth (coins, gold bars, Treasury Bills) can be sent through the mails via Registered Letter. The cost is $3.60 to insure the contents for $500, plus First Class postage. Cost for up to $1,000 is $3.85 plus first class postage, and, if your ship comes in, so to speak, the folks back home can register any amount up to $15 million for mailing.

Registered mail is kept under lock and key, and must be signed for by everyone who handles it, so it tends to be a bit slower than regular First Class mail. You can speed things up somewhat by using Special Delivery, but that takes over only after the letter arrives at its destination city. Express Mail can't be registered. Registered mail can be sent abroad as well as within the U.S., but the indemnity is far smaller—sometimes only a small fraction of the actual cash value. Don't confuse Registered Mail with Certified, which is cheaper but merely establishes proof of delivery. It offers no insurance protection.

After it became clear that we'd get to Fort Lauderdale at least once a year for our hauling and reprovisioning, we decided to open a small savings account there even though we had other accounts for other reasons. This enabled us to cash our own checks or those we received by mail, deposit checks to clear them, and have a local bank reference. A regular passbook account never pays the best interest, but you make up for that in convenience. If you do decide to dot the globe with your savings accounts, as W.C. Fields did, be sure you know what state laws apply. Accounts which are inactive for certain periods revert to the state.

There is one other form of "account" which was invaluable to us. We opened a joint bank account with my parents. The balance in this special, separate account was kept fairly low, to avoid any legal difficulties in case someone died. When we were out of the country, the folks could make our checks "for deposit only" and clear them without having to risk them in overseas mails. They could pay our postage from it, pay important insurance and charge card bills that came while we were beyond reach of the mails, and draw on it any time we asked them to. If there was a family funeral, we asked Mom to buy our flowers from the joint account. On gift-giving occasions, we could specify what we wanted to go where. If the balance got too high, we transferred some of the money to our own account. If it got too low, we could replenish it by check. Thanks to Mom's good bookkeeping, it worked out beautifully for ten years without putting the folks out of pocket for the many favors they did us.

As you've determined by now, there are many ways to keep your cash cloverleaf flowing. Credit cards, travelers checks, and U.S. Bonds are used independently by you alone, and they cost varying amounts both initially and in interest. Money that is mailed or wired to you involves the cooperation of a trusted colleague, but it means your money can stay safely at home or in some high-interest account until you're desperate enough to send for it.

W hen you're cruising foreign countries there are some special snares to watch for. One is that charge-card purchases are computed according to the exchange rate *on the day the merchant turns in his bill*. If there is a big fluctuation in the meantime, you could end up paying a far different price than you signed for.

We always make our overseas exchanges at banks, which figure the rate to the third decimal. Stores and restaurants round off the exchange, often with a very broad pencil and never in your favor. You may do even better on the black market, but we never wanted to take the chance of riling our host government.

When traveling abroad, we stick to better-known brands of travelers checks such as Barclay's and American Express. Check with several banks. Some travelers checks are free. For overseas travel, we buy them in $100 denominations because so many countries put a per-check tax on them. If you cash in ten $10 checks in these countries, the tax is ten times greater than on one $100 check.

If you want to nail down an exchange rate before you go, you can buy travelers checks here in the more popular foreign currencies. You'll lose if the dollar strengthens after you leave, gain if the dollar weakens, but at least you'll know how many pounds or francs you have in your jeans. Any time you're cashing travelers checks, at home or abroad, establish first that yours will be accepted. If you blithely countersign, then learn that the merchant doesn't have the cash to cover it or that he doesn't like the cut of your jib, the check may be ruined.

Another way to transfer funds abroad is through letter of credit,

The navigator's station and chart table often double as the desk for dockside use. If you're not using a chart, you're using a checkbook.

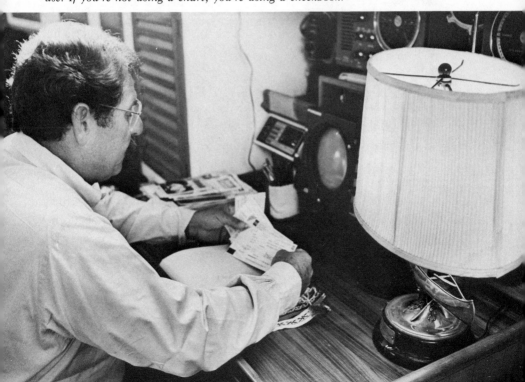

which can be arranged with your local bank. This is especially helpful if you'll be buying your boat overseas or making other large purchases.

Some cruising investors gained greatly by playing exchange rates, especially during the volatile 1970's, by putting their dollars into Swiss francs or Krugerands. Others had to cut short their cruises as the worth of their dollars melted away. Only you can decide how to play the money game. If you do want to bank abroad, Harry Browne's *Guide to Swiss Banks* makes interesting reading.

As you cruise, try to keep pace with your exchange needs. Every time dollars are changed into another currency, you pay for the bank's service. If you leave one country with leftover currency that must be exchanged again in the next, you pay again. This is a special problem in those countries that impose an artificial exchange rate domestically. When you get outside the country, you find that the funds are worth far less than you paid for them. For instance, there was a time when the Bahamian dollar was traded at par with the U.S. dollar within the Bahamas but, if you came home with Bahamian dollars, you lost 15% or more.

When we cross a border, we keep all foreign currencies separate from any remaining U.S. funds. It's easier and safer to deal and think completely in the coin of the current realm, but do fight the "toy money syndrome" which strikes during the first few days of using a new coinage. New money seems unreal, and it's hard to shift gears mentally and use it sparingly.

Most important of all, keep abreast of money trends, no matter how content you are in your island idyll. Interest rates soared during the 1970's while some liveaboards sailed on, their capital languishing in C.D.s paying 6%. It's easy to ignore something so important when your lockers are filled with canned goods, your boat is up to date, and you have few purchases to make.

If you'll be wiped out when the bottom falls out of pork belly futures, of if Wall Street flounders, it may be best to sign over power of attorney to a professional who can manage your portfolio wisely for you. The better you husband your finances, the longer and more comfortably you can live aboard, and cruise.

Chapter 11

Mail Call

~~~~~~

L etters from home let you know you are loved and remembered. Checks come through the mail to keep your liveaboard exchequer afloat. So do bills, business, bad news and good news, spare parts and other mail orders, charts, greetings and gifts. The daily mails transfuse us all as they bring the outside world to anywhere we happen to be. But oh, what a tangled web we weave when we give up an address to go live on a boat. Problems abound, but Gordon and I managed not only to get our mail, we made our living as freelance writers for ten years by mail, without having a mailbox to call our own.

The first thing any liveaboard needs is an address or mail drop. It would be impossible to notify every correspondent every time you move on. We refused to reveal our temporary addresses except in rare cases, and cautioned our parents against giving our ever-changing addresses to anyone. It was a constant struggle to keep our mail going to Alabama when everyone knew we were really in the Bahamas or Keys. We found that once an address is written down, mail goes there forever. It's especially difficult when your closest friends and dearest relatives feel that, while a forwarding address applies to others, you should keep them posted on exactly where you are. It just doesn't work that way and we finally convinced everyone that we had only one address.

You can have a friend or relative handle your mail free, or have a professional (lawyer, secretary, mail service) do it for a fee. The post office can also handle your mail for you. More about that later. Most of the younger liveaboards we know have all their mail sent to their parents; most older liveaboards have one of their children handle their mail.

A third choice, which applies only to those liveaboards who spend all winter in one port and all summer in another, is to notify all your correspondents that your address June through September is Edgartown; October through May, Key West. Stationery printed with dates and both addresses helps people remember where to find you, and the post offices on each end can easily forward any mail that goes to the wrong address at the wrong time.

Both fee and free services have their pluses and minuses. When a trusted friend or relative handles your mail, you can have them weed out things you don't want, pay bills if you're between addresses, and do all sorts of special, individual things. My wonderful parents realized the importance of getting our mail to us as quickly and as cheaply as possible, time after time. Knowing the high cost of sending airmail to us in foreign countries, Mom trimmed every business letter down to the bare bones. When we were underway for weeks at a time, they held our mail. Then, when we phoned or wrote that we had an address they made a special trip to the post office to bundle it all off to us by the quickest means possible. If there was time only for one shot of First Class mail, they sent only that. If we were going to linger longer in port they would send magazines, rejected manuscripts, and other bulk mail. No amount of money can buy the kind of mail forwarding that thinks, cares, and hustles as my folks did for us.

However, we've met liveaboards whose relatives didn't appreciate the importance of keeping the mail flowing. Such liveaboards have languished in port for weeks, waiting for a check or a spare part which a busy relative back home just didn't get around to sending. Even the most willing volunteer may weary of the work involved; even the most faithful relative occasionally gets sick, or busy, or goes on vacation himself.

If you want a professional to handle all or part of your mail, you might approach your bank, stockbroker, lawyer, or a secretarial service. Any of them can provide other helpful services as well, usually at an hourly charge which you must consider when planning your liveaboard budget.

Mail forwarding services, especially those which cater to fulltime wanderers, are another choice. The best ones are on duty all the time either in person or through telephone recordings. Others have post office box addresses and forward your mail less often—which may be enough for your needs.

I talked to three forwarding services, after eliminating from my list those that had only post office box addresses, and one which had a telephone that did not answer. Many times we've walked a long way to find a telephone or waited hours to get a call through on the radiotelephone. I'd want only a forwarding service that was always on duty. If they have no telephone, it means notifying them by mail each time your address changes, and that adds another three to four days to the time it takes your mail to reach you.

Bellevue Avenue Executive Mailboxes (38 Bellevue Ave., Newport, RI 02840) answer the telephone 8-4:30 Eastern Time on weekdays, and at other times have a recording machine which will take your

Mail is particularly important to liveaboards, who usually have no phone. A writing desk can become a favored seat.

message or will tell you whether there is mail in your box. The charge
here is $10 a month plus a postage deposit and a small charge for each
envelope. They'll forward as often as you like, but recommend that it is
cheaper to send your mail in batches rather than every time one letter
trickles in. They'll take delivery of your parcel service packages and will
remail them. And, if you're waiting for something special such as a
check, they'll keep a special eye out for it and will get it to you in one
day via Federal Express.

T.R.A. (710 W. Main Street, Arlington, TX 76012) maintain
near-24-hour telephone service at (817) 261-6072. They're a family
business, with someone home most of the time. Their charge is $40 a
year plus postage, which they'll bill you for in increments of about
$15. Usually they remail three times a week but if you prefer they'll
mail once a week or even less often.

M.C.C.A. (P.O. Box 2870, Estes Park, CO 80517) have a toll-free
number, (800) 525-5304, which is a boon to the roaming liveaboard. If
no one is there to take your call in person, there's a recording machine
which has no time limit, so you can take your time to explain where
you want your mail sent, when. They also charge an annual fee, plus a
small postage deposit.

One drawback to all such services is that all your mail will be
packaged up and remailed. Even First Class mail is re-posted and First
Class postage paid again because, once it is delivered somewhere, the
post office won't accept it back for forwarding. A really reliable friend
or relative, on the other hand, can fill out the required post office
forms each time to have your mail forwarded automatically by them or
can open the mail and re-mail letters without envelopes and other
worthless weight. And, although the post office won't accept once-
delivered mail for forwarding en masse, the occasional letter can be
re-addressed and dropped in a mailbox.

If you'll be gone only for a year or so and want to retain your home
address, set up a trust fund with the local post office. They can't
extend credit so you'll have to keep enough money in the fund to cover
costs. First Class mail is forwarded free; there will be a charge for other
classes. While you can instruct the post office to weed out some junk
mail, they can't be as selective as Mom can in sending one catalog but

not another, a boating magazine but not a gardening weekly. Nor will they usually take instructions by phone, as a friend, mail service, or relative can. Still, the service is free, prompt, professional, and impersonal (a nice feature if you don't want anyone going through your dividend checks or love letters).

There's one other problem we ran into during a period when the post office was forwarding all our mail. They fed our forwarding addresses into a computer, which printed out labels with that address, to be pasted on each batch of mail. Our forwarding address was changing about every two weeks at that time, and occasionally the computer would spit out some old forwarding address instead of the new one! We waited for a week or two in the Carolinas for our mail and eventually learned from our puzzled friends in Vermont that mail for us was pouring in. They thought we were coming back. A smaller post office, one without a computer and where your name would be remembered, is a better choice. You can have a personal relationship with the clerks there, send them a postcard or box of candy once in a while and, in general, get more personal service.

Here are some things we learned while getting our mail on the go within the United States:

1. If you're using General Delivery, choose small towns rather than large cities. Such mail usually goes to the main post office downtown, and that is rarely the post office handiest to the marina. In small towns the walk is shorter, the service more personal. Countless times we've walked into a small post office, given our names, and been greeted by huge grins and a friendly "We've been waiting for you. We have a ton of mail for you!"

2. Try to get an idea of how much mail has been forwarded. Very often we've been given only one bundle of mail but, knowing there was also a parcel or some large envelopes, we asked the postal worker to look again. Usually more mail was found. If several bundles are shipped at once, it's useful to label them, e.g. #1 of 3, and so on.

3. If you're delayed in getting to a new port, send a post card to the postmaster there asking him to hold your mail until you arrive. General Delivery mail can be held for only 15 days. It is then returned to

the sender unless you've given other instructions *in writing*. Postmasters in towns where there are many transient boats are, however, more aware of the kinds of delays and problems encountered by liveaboards. Sometimes a phone call will do, especially if you promise to follow up with a note. Such postmasters will often re-forward the forwarded mail to you if you're stuck in another port.

4. Have your mail forwarder put his return address on each piece of mail. It's easy and inexpensive to do with a rubber stamp or glue-on labels. Then, if the mail does go astray, it will go back to your forwarder instead of the original sender. In a couple of instances we've lost touch completely with an important correspondent because mail went back to him marked "no known address" or something else that made him stop sending mail to our permanent forwarding address.

Another way we've sometimes lost touch is that some correspondents, especially credit cards companies who don't want to lose track of you, instruct the post office to notify them every time you have a new address. So, because your mail has gone to Beaufort for a couple of weeks, Mastercard bills start going there permanently. The only way to fight this, if your mail is being forwarded by the post office, is to give special instructions both to the credit company and to the postmaster.

5. When you leave each address, always leave a forwarding address. If you don't know what your next port will be, leave your permanent address as a forwarding address. If mail straggles in after you leave, and it often does, it will find its way either to you or to your mail handler. Leaving a forwarding address also reminds the boatyard or marina or post office that you have been there and left. We returned to a marina four years later, to find a few pieces of yellow, old (fortunately unimportant) mail still waiting for us!

6. Whenever you order anything by mail, be sure to give a street address. Parcel services can't deliver to post office boxes or General Delivery. Nor can they forward. It's also a good idea to note on the order, "Notify at once if item can't be shipped immediately" because most mail-order outfits automatically back order. The shipment could be made weeks after you leave.

7. Emphasize to your mail forwarder that certified or registered mail should never be signed for if it can be forwarded on the spot. If it

~~~~~~

is signed for, it must be re-registered or re-certified and remailed, which is very expensive.

8. Impress your mail forwarder of the importance of weighing and stamping mail with enough postage. If you're staying at a marina, and something comes "postage due" to the office, a form will be left instructing you to go to the post office—and that can be a long and expensive trip if you haven't a car.

9. Do everything possible to pare down the amount of mail sent to you. Mailing lists are like the Hydra, the mythical creature that grew back two heads for every one that was cut off. When we ordered anything by mail, we noted on the form, "Temporary address; do not place on mailing list." We also let all our magazine subscriptions lapse. It was cheaper to buy them at the newsstand than to pay forwarding postage. Despite our best efforts there were often stacks of catalogues waiting for us at the yard where we were hauled once a year.

10. Carry identification when you go to pick up mail at General Delivery. It's often required and is for your own protection. Even if it isn't requested, however, we print our name on a scrap of paper and show it to the postal clerk. In our early liveaboard years we were sometimes told there was no mail for us after we spoke and spelled our name. We knew mail was there, showed them the name, and the mail was found.

Once you leave U.S. shores, the mail picture gets far more complicated and expensive. Mail is forwarded free (by the post office but not by forwarding services) from the United States to U.S. possessions, Canada, and Mexico. Mail sent to other countries, however, goes at about four times domestic rates. If you have everything forwarded intact, it's an enormous expense. Even if you get only First Class mail, it's costly. If you have a trusted mail forwarder who can separate wheat from chaff, here's where it really pays off. For non-First-Class mail, things can be sent via a special rate called A.O., a kind of second class airmail available to some overseas countries. Surface mail is cheaper still, but can take weeks or even months. Depending on the country, special rates also apply to books and to packets weighing under a certain limit.

Here are some tips on getting your mail after you leave home shores:

1. Mail addressed to Captain Whatsisname, Yacht Soandso, helps get you more attentive service.

2. Regardless of your grievances against the American postal service, you'll find the post worse in most other countries. When you're in one of the "manana" countries, relax and enjoy the slower pace. The more steamed you get about their casual attitude towards mail, the more time it will take them to find yours.

3. We've been in some foreign post offices which were in such chaos we were led to a huge mountain of mail and invited to find ours if we could! After that, we asked my folks to buy tape or peel-off labels in some bright color and to put some on every piece of mail they sent us. Many times we've spotted that wink of color across the room and knew we had mail even when the postal clerk said we had none.

4. While it's helpful to give U.S. post offices your name in writing it's absolutely crucial in foreign countries, especially those where English is not spoken. In Spanish, our V sounds like a B; in German, V is pronounced like F, and even in the English-speaking Bahamas, W's and V's are transposed.

5. When possible, write ahead to a port where you plan to get mail and ask them to hold mail for you, with emphasis on your full name, very clearly printed. We once arrived at Grand Bahama, mail-starved after weeks in unpeopled islands, and called at a hotel/marina for mail. Our precious mail had all been packed off back to the States that morning, after a Mr. and Mrs. Greene had checked out!

6. Advise well-meaning relatives not to send gifts to you in foreign ports unless you've had some experience with the customs situation in that country. Various limits apply, but you may end up paying more than the item is worth by the time you pay duty. A Christmas package sent to us in Nassau involved two trips across town to the customs house, plus $10 duty. Some of our cruising friends who had received food parcels from America or Canada abandoned them when they learned what the duty would be. Other packages don't show up in time, and some never arrive at all. There are bright spots in this picture. One is that packages addressed to "Yacht in Transit" can enter some countries duty-free. Another is that books can be sent duty-free to

most countries, and used items carry a reduced tariff. If, for instance, your family washes the shirt they are sending you for Christmas, it is no longer dutiable as "new." Still, however, you may have to pick it up at customs in those countries where foreign parcels aren't sent through the mail.

7. Your mail drop overseas could be the home or business of a friend, a bank, a boat yard, or Poste Restante. We found it best to arrive first and look things over before sending for our mail. Once we found that our mail was addressed to an island hotel which got mail service only once a week—and then someone had to pick it up at a neighboring island where we couldn't go with our 5½-foot draft. Another time, after we saw that all mail addressed to one marina was tossed into a bin for just anyone to root through, we made other arrangements.

8. If you're cruising the Bahamas, Central America, Baja, or the Caribbean, try to work a deal with a local hotel, freight forwarder, or company that has a U.S. address. Your mail can then be flown in with theirs. Even if you pay them a substantial fee, your mail will probably come quicker, safer, and cheaper than if you get it through the local postal system.

9. Cruising these same, nearby countries, carry a large supply of U.S. stamps and a small postal scale. Countless times we've been able to send mail out of the Bahamas with passing pilots. Since it was weighed, stamped, and ready to drop into any U.S. mailbox, they were glad to do it. It would have been more difficult for them if we had given them money and expected them to stamp the mail. As far as we know, every piece of mail—including dozens of our magazine articles and the entire manuscript for my *The Galley Book* got through month after month, year after year. Incidentally, my method for carrying stamps works well in damp sea air. Make up a "book" by stapling together sheets of waxed paper, and put pages of stamps between each. Otherwise, the glue on stamps gets wet and they stick together. I don't recommend that liveaboards buy stamps in rolls.

10. When you're sending mail from overseas post offices, don't forget that you need *domestic* stamps. Your U.S. stamps aren't good there.

11. Single-sheet aerogrammes, also called International Air Letters,

are a great bargain for international mails and we've always found them to be one or two days faster than airmail letters. You can buy them in any country (and your correspondents can buy them in the U.S. when they write to you) at a few cents less than the normal, half-ounce, airmail rate. Bear in mind that space is limited to what you can write on the one sheet, which folds to form an envelope, and that nothing can be enclosed.

12. Try to acquaint yourself with overseas postal rates so you'll know if you're getting stuck. Postal officials who don't deal commonly with overseas mail are confused by the jumble of various rules and rates that apply. While cruising in England we got in the habit of going to a couple of post offices for quotes—which varied widely for the same parcel sent by the same class mail! This could make a difference for heavy things such as winch or engine parts.

13. It's always important to wrap mail well. When it has to cross national borders, it's even more important. It isn't enough to stuff a pile of magazines into a manila envelope. Magazines travel best when they are rolled in heavy paper, then taped or tied. Or, try a new envelope material called Tyvec. It is absolutely tear-proof and it's worth the extra cost. It's available at office supply stores and stationers.

14. When sending gifts home, stay away from seeds, jewelry made from vegetable or animal sources, foods, and furs unless you know for certain that they can enter the U.S. Tobacco and alcohol are verboten, and so are perfumes valued at more than $5. You can mail gifts of less than $25 retail ($40 from the Virgins, American Samoa, or Guam) duty free, and you can send one $25 gift per recipient per day, "day" being defined as the day the parcels arrive in U.S. Customs. Don't count on merchants or postal officials overseas to know what rules apply. We found that some, such as clerks at the larger post offices in New Zealand, were well versed on mailing to the U.S. In some other countries, though, postal workers simply don't know what rules apply on this end and many merchants are interested only in making a sale, not whether the item will be seized by the U.S. Customs. Send for the booklet *Know Before You Go* from The Department of the Treasury, U.S. Customs Service, Washington, DC 20229.

Chapter 12

Doctor at the Dock

There's one thing worse than having a real gut-wrenching, tooth-grinding, repent-your-sins bellyache and that's having the bellyache far from your family doctor or, worse still, far from any doctor at all. We've taken our share of licks: some cracked ribs, Gorden's bad fall when he landed on his head, several episodes of painful swimmer's ear, some dental debacles. Except for one hospital emergency that happened while we were, providentially, in Fort Lauderdale, most of our illnesses found us somewhere out in Dire Straits, armed with little more than aspirin, Cruex, and ouchless bandages. Injuries and illnesses are things liveaboards fear most. How can you cope?

Before we moved aboard, we kept having terrifying fantasies about falling from the topmast and fracturing a leg in three places, exotic tropical diseases, appendicitis in some foreign port peopled by witch doctors who speak only Toltec, or having malaria on some island where the only doctor is an expatriate American who had been defrocked for habitual drunkenness. Even if you never leave home waters, however, there are special problems for the liveaboard.

In the United States, many doctors no longer accept strangers as patients so, in strange towns, you may have to grovel a bit before anyone will even give you an appointment. When you do see a sawbones, you'll pay a premium for the initial visit because of the time it takes to get your medical history. Everybody wants cash on the barrelhead, which can add to your woes if your Blue Cross card went down with the ship.

As a result, most of us put off office calls until we're desperate, and delay regular check-ups as long as possible. Take heart, though. We've had many good experiences with helpful, caring people. Usually, dockside neighbors were able to steer us to doctors. Once, I phoned a number given to me by a fellow liveaboard, to find that the doctor was on vacation. His receptionist volunteered to call around to find an appointment with a doctor I could reach on foot or by bus. "I know the town," she said cheerfully when I explained that I was a wayfaring stranger. "Besides, you may as well not stand there and feed quarters into the phone." A kind and perceptive lady.

There are a couple of ways to bring some continuity into your liveaboard medical and dental care. It soon became a pattern for us to haul the boat in Fort Lauderdale and provision there before heading for the Keys or Bahamas. So we had all our check-ups there. Some of our friends, who roamed from spot to spot, spent the money to fly to their favorite clinic every year. Any unexpected illnesses had to be dealt with on the go, but their longtime records were always available in one spot.

Once you venture into an isolated island group, down a remote river, or offshore, things get more complicated. When you leave your own country, complications increase and, if there is a language barrier, become downright chaotic.

Let's go back to basics, well before the time comes to start packing your medicine chest with disposable morphine syringes, scalpels, and pliers for performing do-it-yourself molar extractions. First comes preventive medicine. Two of the biggest killers are excessive weight and smoking, and you can cure yourself of both. Have good medical and dental check-ups, and tie up all the little loose ends such as having that suspicious mole removed, your fillings brought up to date, and your blood pressure brought under control. If you've been putting off elective surgery, get it out of the way.

Then talk to your insurance broker to see what can be done about coverage during your liveaboard years. If you'll be leaving your present job and group insurance plan, inquire about converting the policy. It will cost more than you're paying now but you can convert without passing any new physical exam.

We swallowed hard and let our medical insurance lapse. We hoped that our youth (I was 31, Gordon 38 when we moved aboard), our blooming health, and the fact that we'd both come from long lines of long-lived rascals would make it a safe gamble for us. It turned out well, but everyone has to make his own decision.

After a few years, we found a "disaster" policy that begins covering us after we pay the first $5000. Again, the gamble paid off because we've saved more than $5000 in premiums by not having one of those policies that covers every hangnail. With most policies, a couple must pay the family rate which is more than twice the price of two singles. It's a good deal for families; a poorer buy for couples—especially couples who do not include pregnancy among their future medical plans. If you're a couple, look into whether you can qualify for two single policies with different companies.

It's your own decision, but don't rule out medical insurance just because you plan to cruise abroad. When serious or longterm illness strikes, all the liveaboards we've known have fled back to the States for better care and to be nearer families.

Twice I've been treated by doctors in countries which have government medicine, and the experiences were pretty awful, both medically and financially. Other liveaboards, though, have had better experiences abroad, including some excellent medical care for next-to-nothing. However, I don't recommend going to sea with the *sole* plan of sponging off overseas socialized medicine. Not every country gives free medical care to just anyone who grunts up to the trough. In others, one look at the free hospitals will send you scuttling for home on the first Pan Am flight.

Speaking of air evacuation, an insurance policy that costs only about $70 a year is aimed at travelers who want to be flown home in case of illness. For details, contact N.E.A.R., 1900 N. MacArthur, Oklahoma City, OK 73127. In the U.S. you can telephone them toll free at (800) 654-6700.

If you're on a strapped budget and need free care, it's availabe in many areas even in the U.S. Often you'll stumble onto a free glaucoma or diabetes screening, chest X-rays, or blood pressure tests given by some volunteer group. Some cities have free clinics for the needy. Birth control supplies and advice are available through Planned Parenthood. When we needed yellow fever shots, we learned the vaccine was available only at a free county clinic. While they were at it, they threw in smallpox and tetanus shots. When you get immunizations of any kind, get a written record (the World Health Organization uses a yellow card). It's one of the most valuable medical records—if only to keep you from getting the needle more often than is absolutely necessary.

After you've caught up on your medical, dental, and optical needs, and decided on insurance, talk to your doctor about a medical kit that will be the most help in your liveaboard situation. The more remote your voyaging, the more supplies you'll need and the more responsibility you must take for your own medical care.

You now probably have a family doctor who keeps track of your weight and blood pressure, profiles your blood, keeps records on what diseases you've had and what medicines you're taking. The dentist has your X-rays; the opthamologist has your eyeglass prescription and remembers when you had your last glaucoma test. Once you leave your home town you're the only one who will be able to tell a strange physician what shots you've had, the name of those little yellow pills you've been taking for years, what allergies you have, and whether there is anything new and alarming about your weighing X pounds.

After moving aboard, we became much more aware of health— past, present, and future. After a visit to a doctor and sometimes during, we make note of weight, blood pressure, and other things the doctor discovers or says. We also keep files of medical articles that apply to something we've had in the past or diseases common to areas we're in.

In some states, prescriptions are labeled only if the physician gives his OK. We always know what we are taking, if not from the doctor then from the druggist, and we insist on getting the brochure on indications/contraindications that comes with each drug. This information is added to our medical diary.

Our dentist gave us our X-rays and we carry them as we travel. Even though old X-rays don't reveal new problems, mine came in handy in

Fort Lauderdale when a dentist was able to make a tricky diagnosis only by comparing a new picture to an old one. Incidentally, we find a dentist each time by asking for the newest one in town. In smaller places, ask around. In larger cities call the dental society. It's likely that the newcomer will have time for you, will have sparkling new equipment, and the last word about the newest techniques and materials in dentistry.

Among the special things we carried in our medical kit were a medication for fish poisoning, a problem sometimes in the Bahamas even among natives who know which fish to avoid. It's an even greater danger in the Pacific. We also carried high-voltage pain pills, a good selection of bandages and ointments, hexachlorophene soap for skin infections, Lomotil for diarrhea, prescription "uppers" in case we needed help in staying awake during a difficult night passage, antibiotics, aspirin, and assorted other minor remedies. Work out your own list with your doctor.

Two of the most valuable healers in any medical arsenal are heat and cold. They're old-fashioned, but hot water bottles and mustard plasters can still be a great comfort. The water bottle doubles as an enema bag. Few of us are old enough to remember mustard plasters, which burned the skin if you weren't careful. My great-aunt made hers by mixing one tablespoon dry mustard with four tablespoons lard or shortening instead of water, which was usually used, and they were just as effective without irritating. The mixture is spread on a cloth, topped with another thin cloth, and applied to the skin.

Although we had ice in port, we were without it for months at a time so we carried chemical ice packs. You activate them as needed, and they get cold without refrigeration. One source for these and other medical supplies for the adventurer is Indiana Camp Supply, P.O. Box 344, Pittsboro, IN 46167. The company is operated by a physician who has a special interest in first aid for outdoorsmen. The catalogue also lists a toothache kit, sutures, butterfly bandages, immobilization splints, and other items not easily found.

Another catalogue is Edmund Scientific, 101 E. Gloucester Pike, Barrington, NJ 08007, which offers things like a tooth repair kit and instruments for checking ears, nose, blood pressure, and heart. These, plus a good thermometer, will help you to keep tabs on yourself, and to report vital signs to a doctor when you're being treated by radio.

Medical Advisory Systems are one source of professional medical advice by radio, now that the Coast Guard no longer provides this service. You get various manuals, I.D. cards, and other features plus 24-hour medical advice access via VHF and SSB marine operators, or the free 800 telephone number. SSB range is said to be 6,000 miles. Coverage for an individual is $25 a year. Another $20 will buy coverage for another adult and all his or her children under 18. For $10 you can get updated, computerized medical information, and for $45 you can get emergency service for guests. Write MAS' Pleasure Craft Division at Box 193, Chaneyville Junction, Owings, MD 20736 or phone them at (800) 123-4567 for information on how you can sign up.

If you'll be cruising abroad, you may want to join the International Association for Medical Assistance to Travelers, which provides lists of English-speaking doctors in many countries who have done post-graduate work in the U.S., Canada, or Great Britain. Membership is free; medical services are priced about the same as doctor calls in the U.S. In the U.S., write IAMAT at Suite 5620, 350 Fifth Ave., New York, NY 10001. In Canada, 123 Edwards St., Toronto M5G 1G2. In Australia, St. Vincent's Hospital, Victoria Parade, Melbourne 3065. A similar service which is more costly is Intermedic, 777 Third Ave., New York, NY 10017.

Seasickness is something dreaded by anyone who goes to sea, and we've both been decked by it at one time or another. It's hard to separate myth from medicine, but there is a wealth of new treatments as well as lots of folklore. One of the most persistent stories, one I haven't put to the test, is that a dab of Vicks Vapo-Rub in the navel will keep you from getting seasick. There's a new behind-the-ear drug that gives ongoing protection for several days. Called Transderm V, it's a prescription drug. The Acu-Band (P.O. Box 432, Rumson, NJ 07760-0432) uses the acu-pressure principal. It's a wrist strap and is said to put pressure on the spot that prevents nausea. Both these have the advantage of being non-oral. Suppositories are also available for those unlucky souls who can't keep anything down.

In any case, both Gordon and I have trouble only for the first few days out of port. And some people never suffer mal de mer at all. If you're prone to motion sickness, start treatment before you leave the dock or it will probably be too late.

Most of the first-aid manuals I've seen were no help at all to the sailor who is hours, even days, from professional help. One invaluable reference is *The Merck Manual*, published for physicians and difficult reading for the layman. Still, enough can be understood to help you diagnose sicknesses, ask and report the important things when you're getting medical advice by radio, comprehend doctors' orders, and in general get some sort of handle on what's ailing you. *Medicine for Mountaineering* (1977, Mountaineer Books, 719 Pike St., Seattle, WA 98101) is, unexpectedly, also a fine reference guide for sailors. Rarely are doctors on mountaintops, just as there are few doctors at sea, so the book proceeds from the premise that you'll have to deal with problems yourself, at least initially. *The Yachtsman's Emergency Handbook* (Hearst Marine Books) has first aid and other emergency topics alphabetically. Several medical books are offered by BOAT/U.S., 880 S. Pickett St., Alexandria, VA 22304.

Another book for the liveaboard to carry is *The Ship's Medicine Chest and Medical Aid at Sea*. It's published by the Public Health Service and is sold through the Government Printing Office. Since it's written for medical officers aboard ships which do not have doctors aboard, it gives practical, usable advice on treating and recognizing almost anything that could happen aboard. It's a sturdy, hardbound book selling very reasonably at about $15.

The latter book stresses the need for prior training in emergency care, particularly in knowing Cardio-Pulmonary Resuscitation. CPR is a pleasant, easy, and very rewarding course that takes about 12 hours. Although you can read about it time and again, it takes hands-on experience with the special dummies used in training courses to get the rhythm and feel of the exact routines which must be followed. (Don't practice on people; injury can result.) CPR savvy is one of the best gifts you can give yourself, your family, and your crew.

Through the Red Cross in your town you can also sign up for first-aid and advanced first-aid courses. Things have changed greatly since I was a Girl Scout. A good, modern first-aid course does wonders for your self confidence, skills, and ability to communicate by radio when you're asking for medical help.

The roving life can save you money on hospitalization insurance. Rates vary dramatically from one state to another. As long as you won't be living anywhere, try to take out the policy as a resident of one of the cheaper states. The coverage is the same but the rate is based on per diem hospital rates in each area. Make use of friends' and relatives' addresses as necessary, but make sure they are responsible people who will forward the bill in time for you to pay it before the policy expires.

Another advantage is that liveaboards are footloose and free to move on. If there's no heart specialist in Wheezy Valve, sail on to New York or Boston. We've met several retired military people who planned their voyages around ports where they could get free yearly check-ups at the best V.A. facilities.

The biggest medical advantage of all is that the liveaboard is fulfilled and happy. You live the way you want to, where you want. You can go where the air is cleaner, the pace slower, crime more uncommon, the climate more suitable to your needs. And live happily (and healthily) ever after.

Chapter 13

Living Aboard With Kids

W e'd been invited to cruise for a week out of St. Thomas aboard a sportfisherman, crewed by a couple and their 14-year-old son. The boy was doing high school by mail, worked side by side with his parents all day, and, now that he'd completed a college-level course in diesel mechanics, he had taken over the maintenance of the boat's engines, too. He was typical of the dozens of liveaboard children of all ages that Gordon and I have met over the years—poised, resourceful, sea-smart, reliable, and so bronzed and brawny they make city kids look like sissies.

Although there may have been some "boat brats" who turned out rebellious or stupid, we never met one. Nor have we heard of a liveaboard child who, returning to public school after mail-order schooling, wasn't with or ahead of the rest of the class. In every liveaboard family—at least those who cruise as a way of life—there is a quality of cooperation, communication, and pioneer inter- dependence that one seldom sees ashore. The kids aren't necessarily angels, work horses, or geniuses but they are all, in some way, special.

There was the couple with five sons, aboard *Firebird*. And the young doctor, his internship completed, who took a year to cruise the Bahamas aboard a 25-footer with his wife and adorable three-year-old girl. And the Miami accountant who, ready to move his family away from the city, spent a year in the Bahamas with his wife, son, and daughter before taking up a new life in central Florida. And the Vermont couple, both teachers, who auctioned off everything they owned to buy a boat that they and their two girls, ages five and seven, could live on.

163

We met them at Hawks Nest in the Bahamas. And the cutest sight I've seen in years of boating—the very blond couple who had just sailed in from Sweden. On deck were two toddling towheads wearing nothing but faded orange life jackets, their little bottoms brown as cub bears.

There was the Long Island couple who got sick of the city, and sailed off aboard a 72-foot schooner with their seven children. The baby was still in diapers. We caught up with them about five years later in the Bahamas, where they were now living in a magnificent houseboat they had built ashore. On the day we met, Age 12 was grinding the valves on somebody's car while the older girls rowed around the harbor taking orders for home-baked goods which they would deliver early the next morning. Two younger children were out spearfishing for dinner, both for the family and for their pet osprey. Mother was washing, and washing, and washing. Dad was bulldozing a runway on one of the islands. We stayed for a superb dinner, cooked by whatever children whose turn it happened to be. After the table was cleared, the kids showed off their projects: model planes, a kit radio one of them was building, needlework, carpentry—all practical skills which were giving them pleasure now and would for a lifetime.

Fitting Kids In

What is needed to live aboard with children? A couple of things are obvious: safety and room for them. Although four people need more boat than two people do, even this varies with the family. Wayne Carpenter, whose name is well known to sailors because he has edited both *Sea* and *Rudder* magazines, lived aboard and cruised extensively aboard a Northsea 27 with his wife, two daughters, *and* mother-in-law! The young couple and pre-schooler aboard the 25-footer were contented as clams—far moreso than another couple living alone on their 34-footer. It is nice though, to have a bunk for each child, his own stowage space for toys and hobbies, and a place where school-age children can do their lessons each day.

Money? Well, one does need to feed, clothe, doctor, and educate children, but all the liveaboard parents I've met haven't looked at their children as a financial burden any more than Grandpa Walton did. In a subsistence economy, children are wealth. By the time they are eight

The Rhodes-designed sloop Renova *is home for the small girl below. Note the netting below the lifelines.*

At 45 feet, Renova *makes a comfortable year round home for a family of three.*

This is a child's berth. Notice the voracious reading that takes place here.

years old, most liveaboard kids stand their own watches, capably. They help with the fishing and foraging, sanding and sailing. In short, they carry their own weight. Many of them earn money by hiring out to other boats, or by selling a skill, or their own sprouts, or baked goods.

Safety

When I asked a Halifax friend his secret for peace of mind when living aboard with his two pre-schoolers, he summed up very simply "Constant supervision." When it comes to safety for children aboard, I can't improve on that except to suggest a sort of buddy system in which both parents always know which parent is supposed to be watching the baby at any given moment. One liveaboard mother told me that she and her husband knew every minute who was responsible for the helm and who for the baby. They left no margin for those I-thought-he-was-with-you tragedies.

Most marine catalogues sell sturdy nylon netting which liveaboard parents put around lifelines to keep little ones from falling overboard. (On boats without babies it's sometimes used to keep sails from slipping through the lifelines, or to form a catch-all between hulls of a multi-hull, or under a long bowsprit.) It's also ideal for surrounding a bunk, turning it into a crib and playpen. When my friend Caroline brought her new baby home to the boat, she attached the netting securely under the mattress and put hooks overhead. When the netting wasn't wanted, it could be tucked under the mattress. To corral the baby, she hooked the net securely to the overhead. It kept the infant from falling out of the bunk and later, when he reached playpen age, the roomy bunk with its net walls filled that role, too.

Most of us think of rails and nets, or a cozy quarterberth, to keep children from falling out of bed. But make sure that nothing can fall down on them when things get topsy-turvy.

Netting running athwartships gives a baby a sense of his own place aboard, and lets him see what's going on elsewhere while being safely restrained.

For children too small to wear a life preserver whenever they're abovedeck, a strong harness with a tether snapshackeled to a stay is a good idea.

If you shop marine stores and catalogues, you'll find a good selection of life jackets in small sizes, including some models designed for infants. Most of the liveaboard kids I've known have worn their PFD's as routinely as diapers. Keep in mind, though, that life vests can lose their flotation over the years. When yours become sun-faded, hard, or holed, replace them. One other precaution, important to everyone but particularly to tender young skin, is to protect little ones against sunburn, windburn, and eye damage from glare.

Playtime

By shopping marine catalogues you'll find special versions of games for boating families. Magnetic or other nonskid cards and the more popular board games are sold. The new electronic games such as Merlin are compact, versatile, and fun for all ages. A flute or harmonica can provide hours of fun for the musical child; a guitar or uke is even better. If you have more than one or two children aboard, enough to make up a "cast," buy a book of children's plays and let them put on "radio shows" through a portable tape recorder. You can never have too many books, puzzles, and word games.

Whittling, macramé, scrimshaw, model building, painting, and needlepoint are traditional skills, creative and compact. A child interested in sewing can use the skill to make courtesy flags while the family are underway to each new country. Ham radio is one of the most absorbing and useful liveaboard hobbies, and I've met some families who were all ham operators, including the older children. With the help of cassette tapes, a how-to book, and shortwave radio, the whole family can learn new languages before reaching foreign ports. Toys which liveaboards should avoid are: marbles, which can cost a hurrying crewman his footing if they go astray; clay, which is just too messy for the close confines of boat living; and anything made of glass or brittle plastic that can break into sharp-edged shards.

Education

A few years ago, all elementary education for liveaboards boiled down to three words: The Calvert System. Those three words are still very important, but in recent years a quiet trend in American education has taken many children—not just movie stars and boat kids—out of public schools. Parents on the far right find community schools too liberal; liberals find neighborhood schools too restrictive. According to the Wall Street Journal, the Census Bureau estimates that about 1% of the nation's grade-school-age kids aren't in school—a total of about 320,000 children.

For families who live on boats, this means not just a larger choice of mail-order courses, but books and organizations and support systems that were never available to the liveaboard subculture before. One of the leaders of the movement is John Holt, author of *Why Children Fail*. His book *Teach Your Own* is available for $12.50 plus 75 cents postage from Holt Associates Inc., 729 Boylston St., Boston, MA 02116.

Holt also publishes a bi-monthly newsletter which has more than 4,000 subscribers around the world. Titled "Growing Without Schooling" the newsletter is $2.50 per issue, or $30 for 18 issues. Group rates are also available. Included are letters from parents who explain why they took their children out of school, articles on how people learn, and information on how to minimize your legal problems when dealing with bureaucrats. Invaluable to the teacher-parent are Holt's continuing updates on sources of learning materials, and directories of people, schools, and allies of the movement. Through one directory, for instance, liveaboard parents can find pen pals for their children among other un-enrolled children who live ashore.

Holt's mail order book list includes good reading for children of all ages, plus books helpful to home-teacher parents, reference books, and special documents such as a photocopy of a famous Massachusetts Superior Court Case favoring home education. I've never run into a liveaboard family who were being hassled because their children didn't attend school, but it's always a possibility—especially if you don't keep moving briskly. The one trouble liveaboards may have is in enrolling their children in public schools while living at a marina. If possible, use a street address and keep a low profile about your floating home. For reasons I don't understand, some communities accept, without question, children who live in mobile homes whose parents do not own property, but not liveaboard kids whose parents are probably paying more in dock rent than the mobile home parents are paying to rent their trailer lot.

Mail-Order Schooling

One of the most comprehensive home study programs is the Home Study Institute, 6940 Carroll Ave., Takoma Park, MD 20912. Connected with the Seventh Day Adventists, the institute is accredited by the National Home Study Council, and is a member of the National University Extension Association and the International Council for Correspondence Education. It's approved by the Maryland State Department of Education for kindergarten, elementary and secondary, and there are branches in Australia, Brazil, Switzerland, Singapore, Argentina, England, India, and South Africa.

At this writing, kindergarten tuition is $25, grades one through six are $160 each for all subjects, high school $150 per unit, and college $50 per semester hour. All prices are plus books, workbooks, shipping charges, registration and other miscellaneous fees that are outlined in the free brochure which they send on request. There is a full range of academic courses in the arts, humanities, and sciences.

If you want Sunday School lessons for your children, one source I can recommend is Concordia Publishing House, 3558 S. Jefferson Ave., St. Louis, MO 63118. For about $10 per quarter, you get student activity packets, teachers packets and guides, and a Bible study guide. Materials include all sorts of things to do and see, and even the occasional record to listen to. Emphasis is evangelical Christian (Lutheran).

The Calvert School, Tuscany Rd., Baltimore, MD 21210, is where all the liveaboard children I've met were taking their mail-order schooling, and I've never met a parent who didn't praise it to the skies. In each instance, children were able to keep pace with their age group when they went back to regular school, and some kids we've met have alternated between the two types of schooling a couple of times. Curriculum is kindergarten through eighth grade. The school is approved by the Maryland Department of Education and is a member of the Educational Records Bureau.

At this writing, kindergarten costs $135. For grades one through four you'll pay $235 plus another $120 for the advisory teaching service. Grades five through eight cost $255 plus $120 and $130 for advisory teaching service. Although you can order the courses without advisory teaching, Calvert can't furnish transcripts of grades to other schools unless you do. If you opt for the service, which Calvert strongly recommends, a professional teacher will grade papers, comment on the child's work, make suggestions, and advise the home teacher. When the course is completed, the child gets a certificate. Tuition costs include normal shipping (a typical course weighs about 21 pounds) but overseas airmail shipping is extra. All fees are paid in advance.

The Calvert brochure emphasizes that the program is designed for the parent with no teaching experience. Courses are planned to take a nine-month school year but the student can work as quickly or slowly as he wishes as long as the course is completed within two years. Study must begin with the first lesson; there's no provision for starting mid-term even though you can enroll at any time. The school is open year 'round. The pupil will probably work, say the Calvert folks, about five days a week for two to five hours a day.

For current rates, and a rundown of what courses are offered for your children's grade, write Calvert.

Once your children get to the high school level, things get a bit more complicated. Even the most ardent cruisers often dock during the nine-month school year so their teenage children can enjoy the socialization and extracurricular activities that conventional schools offer. Still, there are mail-order high school diplomas available. Just shop carefully to make sure your child can get into the college of choice, based on the high school course you're buying.

The Home Study Institute, listed above, offers a full high school diploma program. Some state colleges and universities offer high school courses by mail. Boarding schools are the answer for some families, and a number of them advertise in *Good Housekeeping* Magazine. Two schools which specialize in people who want to finish high school at home are Cambridge Academy, 1553 N.E. Arch Ave., Jensen Beach, FL 33457, and the American School, 850 E. 58th St., Chicago, IL 60637.

The latter costs from $339 for one year to about $640 for four years of high school. Monthly payments can be made. Two courses, general and college preparatory, are available and both diplomas are accepted by the Army, Navy, and Civil Service. The school is accredited by the North Central Association of Colleges and Schools, and the Accrediting Commission of the National Home Study Council. It's certified by the Illinois Board of Education as a private high school and the curriculum includes shop topics such as blueprint reading and carpentry, automotive and diesel courses, electronics, drafting, and woodworking as well as English, languages, science, social studies and other basics.

At the college level, there are a numer of choices. The CLEP (College Level Examination Program) establishes one's knowledge in a given subject on the basis of a test which is available at 700 places around the U.S. for about $20 per subject. Different colleges have their own idea of a passing mark, and how many CLEP exams they'll allow towards a college degree. For information on how these tests work, write College Board Publications Orders, Box 2815, Princeton, NJ 08541. Another way women can get credit for what they have learned outside school walls is to take a test. The program is aimed primarily at older women who want to return to college or the workplace but could also apply to the liveaboard woman of any age who wants to get a college degree. The tests establish how much she has learned through homemaking and volunteer jobs, and many colleges give some credits on the basis of test scores. A workbook is available for $3 from Accrediting Women's Competencies, Educational Testing Service, Princeton, NJ 08541.

A number of external degree programs are available. For information write to the U.S. Office of Education, 400 Maryland Ave., SW, Washington, DC 20202, or to University Without Walls, Antioch College, Yellow Springs, OH 45387. There are also extension courses, summer courses, and even television courses through which college credit can be earned. If you're serious about earning a degree, be sure to get expert counseling from the beginning because not all credits can be transferred or recognized towards a degree. To avoid any loss of time, money, and credits it's best to start with one college and carry through according to its specific requirements.

Do You Want
a Liveaboard Pet?

coc

I f you love pets and have them in your home, you'll continue to
want the companionship and help of a pet when you live on a boat.
Or will you? Before you run down to the pet shop, think about the
pro's and con's of having a dog or cat on a boat.

On the plus side, an animal is usually a faithful friend, entertainment for the whole family, a conversation-starter with strangers, and a
very practical accessory. One single-hander found that his dog woke
him in plenty of time to take stock of approaching freighters and
change course if necessary. Dogs and cats have wakened sleeping
families in time to save them from fire. Big dogs have thwarted break-
ins, even small dogs can warn you of unwelcome boarders, and cats are
the most effective mousetraps on the market.

There are problems, both for you and for the pet. Some marinas
won't accept liveaboards with pets. You have to walk the dog in all
weather, which may mean walking well inland from the dock to find a
suitable place, or rowing the dog ashore. (However, we once anchored
near a boat with a German Shepherd that had been trained to jump
overboard, swim to the island, do his duty, then swim back.)

You're living in close quarters, so a pet means less room and more
odors—sometimes smells may be so compelling that your guests are
aghast. Pets make extra cleaning problems when they track sand and
salt water aboard, spill food, shed hair, or do gymnastics in the litter-
box. Some foreign countries require that pets be quarantined, causing
delays and expense. It costs money to feed a pet, get medical care, and
pay for whatever grooming is necessary. The pet can't go everywhere

with you, which means leaving it alone aboard or, for long trips ashore, paying for kennel care. A cat with a yen to sharpen its claws, or a teething puppy, can gnaw through a fortune in custom upholstery or nylon line in two and a half seconds.

Pets have minds of their own, and we've seen many liveaboards whose schedules had to be changed because a dog or cat (usually a cat) wandered off. Some of these pet owners finally gave up and went on their way. Some looked for weeks, advertised, offered rewards, and never did find the pet. One searched the bush on a Bahamian island for days, and finally found his cat caught in a hole, nearly starved.

There are problems for the pet too. The list of hurt, missing, and injured liveaboard pets is a long and sad one. We once found a ship's cat nearly dead of dehydration because she had been licking her salt-covered fur, but could not find fresh water.

We've been there, or have heard firsthand, about a dozen pets that have fallen overboard. One was eaten by a shark, many were never seen again, one had to be destroyed. One adorable pup was missing and assumed stolen. Few breeds of dogs are sure-footed enough to be safe on the open sea, and even cats can fall overboard. One was asleep

Ship's cat cools off in the shade of the awning on a hot day.

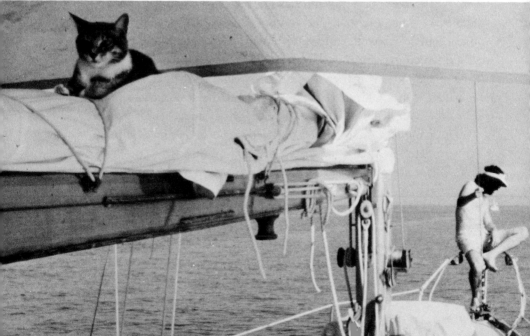

in a sail on deck when suddenly the sail was raised, slinging the cat a boat length ahead. Fortunately the owner was able to fish it out as the boat sailed past. One couple got up one morning to find their kitten clinging to the outboard rudder, and mewing pathetically. It had fallen over during the night and couldn't climb back aboard.

One of the most diabolical discomforts suffered by boating pets occurs because most can't use a marine head (we have seen cats, however, that could). Underway, well-trained animals suffer for hours because the part of the deck they had been taught to use is awash, or because the owners ran out of the brand of litter, or newspaper, or carpeting, which the animal had been taught to use.

Only you can decide whether the service and friendship of a pet will be worth the problems to both the pet and to you. If you do decide to add a dog or cat to your liveaboard family, here are some suggestions.

Health and Well-Being

See a veterinarian about the shots and medications the pet will need for every area you plan to cruise. The shots, and the papers proving the pet has them, are invaluable in foreign ports. Also, you may need heartworm pills or advice about pet illnesses that aren't a problem in home port, but may be wherever you're going. Plague has been going around in the West, fleas in Florida outwit the usual remedies, and ticks can transmit unsavory fevers to pet owners.

Ask your vet for a motion sickness remedy in case it's needed. In our travels we've encountered two cats that got miserably seasick. One merely behaved as humans do. The other had such balance problems underway, it was constantly being flung around the boat, landing on the most inconvenient portions of its anatomy. You may always want to carry some sort of transquilizers for your pet. A large dog, going berserk at the wrong time, can fill a small boat very quickly.

Try to have a comfortable, secure nest where the animal can rest, and be well supported, in rough seas. Sturdy, thick, beanbag-type pet beds are sold by L.L. Bean, Freeport, ME 04033 and Cabela's, 812-13th Ave., Sydney, NE 69162. Both offer free catalogues. Bean is an outfitter for all outdoors sports; Cabela's specializes in fishing and hunting gear. Through them you can also get an automatic dog watering device that attaches to a half-inch pipe, a useful addition if you're living at a dock.

If you can, devise a way for your pet to get back aboard if he falls over. Most cats can simply climb back if you suspend a scrap of heavy carpeting over the side.

Consider a life jacket for your dog, even if he is a good swimmer. The dog's instinct is to stay with the boat, even if he could save himself by swimming to a nearby shore. We were once visiting a boat at a Nassau marina when other guests aboard looked over at their own boat and saw their dog go over the side. The dog ignored their commands to swim to the boat we were on, so she could be lifted aboard. Instead she continued to stay near her boat-home, fighting the swift current, and becoming more and more exhausted. Finally the owner, a strong swimmer, jumped in and rescued the pet. We've seen similar scenes several times since, each time with a happy ending only because someone saw the dog go overboard.

Keeping Track

When you're on the go all the time, a neck tag isn't enough to get a lost pet back to you because it could take weeks to trace a number back to your home port and then to your present port. Look in pet shops for a name tag that has a capsule or slide-in label for easy changing. Then each time you move on, revise it with the name of your present marina and the number of the slip.

If all your cruising will be within the Americas, consider joining the Pet Switchboard, which keeps a record of your pet's medical history and how to reach you. The pet wears a tag bearing his registration number, and a toll-free number to be called by anyone who finds your lost or injured pet. Through this clearing-house, you and your pet can be reunited almost at once. For information, write Kathy Gilroy, Box 105, Lombard IL 60148.

Special Euipment

Non-skid Yachting Tableware vegetable dishes are ideal for feeding and watering pets. They're sold in most marine stores and catalogues.

Such outlets also sell non-skid table mats which can be placed under the feeding area. Pet shops and the Sears catalogue offer a good selection of harnesses, leashes, and tethers. Sears sells a reel-type leash that attaches to a stake in the ground and gives the pet a 15-foot radius.

Training

If your dog is a free spirit, it may be wise for your safety and his to invest the time and money in a good obedience course. The time could come when your command to "stay" or "come" or "fetch" could save his life. We were on a midwestern river just after a boat had blown up. Everyone had jumped overboard in time, except for the dog who had other plans. The family survived; the dog did not. If you want an attack dog, that also requires special training. Spaying and neutering ing are also good temper-tamers.

Good Manners

We once stopped at a marina that banned all pets because one guest, years before, had washed a dog in the shower and clogged the drain with dog hair. While you may see no objection to bathing with or after a dog, others may not feel this way. Use a bucket, hose, or inflatable child-size swimming pool.

Your pet's barking or meowing may be music to your ears, but to marina owners it can be the swan song for liveaboard pets. We once spent a month at a marina in the Florida Keys where our neighbors' dog began howling the moment they left the boat. She didn't stop until her owner's step was heard on the dock. We dreaded their nights out.

It goes without saying that the pet shouldn't be allowed to mess on the dock, yet I've seen dog owners stand and watch while a leg was lifted on our dock lines. Be as conscientious about liquid waste as solid. If you live at one dock month in and month out, you may want to invest in a doggie septic tank which is installed permanently in the ground. It's a clean, ecologically acceptable way to dispose of pet waste, and it's found in the Sears catalogue. Scoops are found in catalogues and pet shops. Whatever good, pet-owner manners you had ashore, double them when you move aboard to make sure you and your pet will be able to find dock space in the future.

Insurance

Could you lose your shirt (or your boat) because your dog bites an innocent passerby, or your cat slashes a playful child? Homeowners' insurance usually covers such special liabilities but your boat insurance probably does not. Talk to your marine insurance agent. If he can't add this coverage to your boating policy you may be able to find an independent broker who can write a special policy.

Adopting a Pet Abroad

Every year sailors come home with adorable pets they've found abroad, only to find that they can't be brought into the country. Sometimes it's because the animal or bird is on the endangered species list; other times it's because the pet is a type that can carry certain diseases to other pets or humans. Since some exotic animals and birds cost a great deal, it can be an economic shock as well as a personal one to have your beloved wombat or warbler confiscated at the docks by an angry customs man. If you're planning on making a large financial (or emotional) investment in a foreign critter, write home for current information from the U.S.D.A. Plant and Animal Inspection Dept., Washington, DC 20229; the U.S. Public Health Service Center for Disease Control, 1600 Clifton Rd. NE, Atlanta, GA 30333; and the U.S. Fish and Wildlife Service, Dept. of the Interior, C Street between 18th and 19th N.W., Washington, DC 20240.

Even though you get a clearance from one agency there is a chance that another would forbid the import for another reason. Even though the import is permitted today, it may be denied by the time you make port because of a new disease scare. And, if you bring in a varmint that is worth more than $250 you'll need a customs broker to handle the deal for you. There's hardly a problem if you stick to less expensive and more common pets, and if you follow customs instructions for papers, shots, and quarantine. By writing ahead for these instructions, and getting all the paperwork done by a veterinarian in the pet's home country, you avoid delays when you come back to U.S. shores.

Chapter **15**

Living Aboard
With the Laundry

⟨⟨⟨

One of my favorite stories deals with a friend who used to live
aboard. Every time she shows a guest her new home ashore she
pauses at the washing machine and says, "And this is the washer" as
she showers it with kisses. Only another liveaboard can understand.
Among the things I missed most while living aboard were the washer
and dryer. If you have a boat large enough, with sufficient water for
conventional laundry facilities, you can skip this chapter.

From the first night aboard when you take off your socks, you have a
laundry problem. Where do you put it? How do you wash it? How do
you dry it? There are many different answers to these questions, depending on where you are and what shoreside facilities are available.
I've taken laundry to dinner parties (at the kind invitation of understanding friends), lugged it on foot to laundromats as far as 5 miles
away, washed and dried it in marina laundromats, and washed it by
hand many times. I've washed it in sea water, sulphur water, brackish
water, village well water, water left over from rinsing the dishes, and in
water from abandoned island cisterns. I've dried it on the lifelines, on
island bushes, on halyards, and in commercial dryers.

Probably the first shock to liveaboards is to find, on that first night
when they're holding their dirty socks, that everything has been
meticulously stowed. Every locker is full, and there is no place for the
dirty clothes. Think it through ahead of time, saving a spot that will get
good air circulation so things won't mildew before you get a chance to
wash them. The longer and more remote your cruises are, the more
space you will need for stowing dirty clothes.

179

Because our boat was small by liveaboard standards, we couldn't spare a locker but settled for two shopping-bag-size poplin bags which were hung in the head. We put white clothes in one, colored clothes in the other. I put detergent powder into them both before leaving for the coin laundry, then threw clothes, soap, and empty bags into two washing machines. On longer cruises, when laundry sometimes had to wait a month for attention, soiled sheets were bundled up and placed in lockers as canned goods were used up.

Here are some suggestions for the details of laundry. Keep plenty of coins handy. Don't be bashful about using lots of washers at once, so you can do all your laundry in the time it takes to do one load. Minimize the laundry aids (liquid bleach, fabric softeners, spray-on stain removers) you depend on, because they must be lugged to the machines with you. Stains can be pre-treated before you leave the boat. Detergent, as mentioned before, can be sprinkled into the bag with the clothes. So can powdered bleaches. (If the clothes are delicate, or the least bit damp, put the powders in a disposable sandwich bag so they don't touch the clothes.) A couple of fabric softener sheets can be tucked into your pocket. (They go into the dryer.) After you've dumped everything into the machines, you can leave empty-handed to do other errands. Don't leave your clothes in the coin laundry after machines stop. Theft is a problem. An impatient customer might (and has the right to) take your clothes out of the dryer and dump them anywhere. Unless you use the same machines regularly, and can depend on them, buy detergents that work in cold water. I've encountered many coin laundries where no hot water was available. In others, water was so hot I could not even use the Warm setting and had to use Cold. Don't crumple soiled clothes into you hamper or laundry bag. If you fold and roll them, as you do when putting them away clean, they'll take up less space and will wrinkle less.

Although boating vacationers might scoff at the idea of carrying an iron, I recommend one for the liveaboard. I have a compact, dual-voltage travel iron with folding handle, but you might have room for a conventional iron. Our cotton curtains were washed, ironed, and lightly starched about twice a year, and you may also want to fuss over placemats and napkins or other fancies for special occasions. My tabletop ironing is done on a folded bath towel. Tabletop ironing boards are readily available, as is a shiny-faced pad called the Daily Press which provides both insulation to your table, and a reflective heat to speed your ironing.

If you need to wash things by hand, it can be accomplished in many different ways: let the clothes roll around in a lidded garbage pail and soapy water; use a bucket; wash in a child-size, inflatable swimming pool (it's better than a bucket for large items such as sheets). You can scrub with a washboard, your hands, or—my favorite—a toilet plunger. A ten-minute soak softens dirt, but longer than that, say some experts, is counter-productive.

If you'll be doing laundry by hand often, try to find a hand-operated wringer. Getting the water out is as important as getting it into the clothes. The Sears catalogue no longer lists wringers or even wringer

Inflatable, child-size swimming pools are ideal for washing clothes on the dock.

washers, but you may be able to scavenge one from a used furniture store. If you can't find a roller-type wringer, let clothes drip rather than twisting as hard as you can, or wear will be rapid.

Salt water can be used for washing clothes, with all sorts of liquid detergents. Powders and bar soaps, however, don't work. Liquids—especially dishwashing soaps—make suds, and more suds, so I prefer the low-suds liquids such as Dynamo or Era. Rinse several times, then use at least one fresh-water rinse with a fabric softener. If you can't spare that much fresh water, don't wash! The salt will stay behind after the clothes dry, and it will continue to draw water out of the air. The result is dampish clothes and sheets, and a clammy smell in your linen locker.

There's one other solution to the laundry problem and I wrote about it years ago. Simply throw things away. When we were in port, with ready access to coin laundries, I set aside garments and linens when it became obvious that they were near the end of the road. By the time we set out for the wilds again, I had a good supply of sheets, towels, dish towels and underwear that was clean, folded, respectable, but one wearing away from the rag bag.

At sea, each of these items was used or worn until it was soiled, then relegated to the rag bin. My conscience was clear. The clothes had a long and useful life; now they were resurrected as oil wipers and scrub cloths, which are always needed aboard. The only difference was that I timed their demise to coincide with times when we were short on water or time or both.

One other laundry tip that applies to liveaboards is that clothes should be rotated often because they seem to develop odd stains—not just mildew but other discolorations that seem to be caused by sea air. If you have some Sunday-best things that are brought out only rarely, or linens that you're saving for your grandchildren, launder them at least once a year even if you haven't used them. Never put anything away after it has been worn or used, no matter how clean it may seem, because stains and soil appear as if from nowhere. And never stow anything salty with or near your clean, dry clothes. Foul weather gear, and towels used after swimming in the sea, should be kept separately.

Chapter 16

Making a Living
While Living Aboard

To be honest, most of the *cruising* liveaboards we have met over the years have had some sort of independent income. Many had done well in business, sold out, invested the money, and were living quite lavishly on the income. Many others had made their fortunes in real estate; some were retiring young after twenty years in the military. Some, like ourselves, were able to keep on the move and earn along the way.

Then there are the dockside liveaboards who go to work like everyone else. Although they are saving to go cruising someday, they continue as secretaries, salesmen, sign painters, and teachers. There are also those liveaboards who work until they have a small nestegg, move on until the funds are gone, work again, move on again—year after year.

A few words of caution about working abroad. Any time you're outside your own country, you may need a special permit to work. If you're caught without it, it can mean expulsion or worse. If you plan to use your boat for hire in U.S. waters, you need a U.S. Coast Guard inspection, and a captain's license. In other countries there are other conditions to fulfill. Mexico and the Bahamas have been especially sticky about foreign charter boats.

If you'll be using your boat commercially, your insurance company needs to know about it, or your policy could be voided just when you need it most.

For those who must work, and yet don't want to settle down to one dock, there are a number of ways to make a living. 183

Stateroom and office, with a view of the water.

Publishing

Writing is one of the most popular liveaboard occupations because you can mail manuscripts from anywhere in the world, work at your own pace, and make money by writing about your adventures. Our writing is the sole source of income for my husband Gordon and myself, and we specialize in a variety of subjects from boating and boat cookery to how-to, travel, aviation, and general assignment. Some well-known authors admired by boating folks and landlubbers alike, have been liveaboards: Lyn and Larry Pardey, Tristan Jones, John D. MacDonald, Donald Hamilton. Others don't have national reputations, but have a solid income from a special writing field such as boating, science fiction, race coverage, business, survival, romance novels. One of my friends, who is bilingual, bums around the world doing translations, covering races, and helping with yacht deliveries.

It would take another book to say all I'd need to in guiding you to a liveaboard income from writing, but there are some general recommendations. One is that this is not the place to pioneer your writing career. Freelancing, even for the former newspaper or magazine staffer, is a cold and cruel outpost. Try it only if you have enough money to last six months until the checks start rolling in. If you'll be writing a book or tackling some other major project, your savings will have to last a year or two before you start harvesting writing profits.

Don't imagine, though, that living on a boat will suddenly spark that novel you've never gotten around to writing. If you've written professionally before, you can do it on a boat. If you haven't paid your dues ashore, it will be more difficult after you move aboard.

In addition to magazine and book writing, some liveaboards have written and published books which they sell themselves. Although you do all the work of publishing and promoting the book, and pay for the printing, you keep all the profits. Our friends Diana and Bill lived in Hawaii for a year, did a book which is still one of the island's best-selling guides, and continue to collect royalties on it.

There are also liveaboards who make a living publishing newsletters and magazines. Peter Smyth, who edited *Motor Boating and Sailing Magazine*, then *Motorboat* magazine, moved aboard his boat *Great Expectations*, chugged to Florida, and has made a success of a beautiful little magazine called *Florida Waterways*.

There are some liveaboard writers who make only part of their living through writing and the rest through chartering, delivering boats, lecturing, films, teaching. It all adds up to enough income to keep them from having to nail down jobs ashore.

For more information on learning to write and publish, get a catalogue of books published by Writers's Digest Books, 9933 Alliance Rd., Cincinnati, OH 45242. A good librarian can steer you to other books about a special field of writing that interests you.

Chartering

Chartering, like writing, sounds like an easy and romantic way to make hay while the sun shines but there are many snags. At best, you may hate having to put up with perfect strangers (usually less than perfect) aboard your boat. At worst, you could flop completely in the tough, tight, cutthroat competition of today's charter field. If you're an independent boat trying to make a living, you'll be competing not only with other hungry liveaboards but with people who use their charter boats as tax write-offs, and with bareboat operations which are cheaper than your crewed boat.

Chartering, however, has far more variations than most people realize and you may be able to work an angle. It might mean collecting passengers to go around the world or on some other exciting journey. Other charter skippers call it a "learn to cruise" experience and charge their guests a fat fee for the privilege of sanding, scraping, dishwashing, and standing watch. Some charter skippers tie in with a hotel, which does the booking for them. Some liveaboards charter only by the day, to avoid having overnight guests aboard.

One couple charter their sportfisherman by day and, when they don't have enough guests to meet their bills, they go fishing themselves and sell the fish. Some specialize in elegant entertaining, offering sunset dinners, corporate cocktail parties, or lavish brunches aboard. Some do live charters, sightseeing charters, research charters. Success hinges on your being an expert at boating, business, and promotion.

For a how-to charter book written by a longtime charter expert, read *The Charter Game*, by Ross Norgrove (International Marine Publishing).

Handyman Work

If you can fix things, you'll always be able to make a living on the water, with or without a work permit, social security card, or other hassle. It's been my observation that the two repairs most in demand are electronics and refrigeration. Even those resourceful, do-it-yourself liveaboards who do most of their own work usually don't have the special equipment needed to do repairs and maintenance in these areas. If you have the expertise and the required tools and test equipment, my guess is that you'll find business in almost any harbor in the world where cruising folks gather. There is also steady demand ashore, at least in the Bahamas, for anyone who can repair refrigerators, freezers, ice makers, and air conditioners.

Arts and Crafts

If you're very talented in one of these areas, you can pick up pocket money—and sometimes more than a pocketful. One liveaboard used her sewing machine to make hats and ditty bags which sold to neighboring boats as briskly as they did to meandering docksiders. Another woman did macramé, taught her children, and the three of them sold their wares. Several liveaboards I've known have used their on-board, heavy-duty sewing machines to do custom canvas work for boating neighbors. All of them had all the work they could handle in any port they ended up in. Lots of sales happen naturally, in the course of cruising. To step up the business, plug into waterfront flea markets and craft fairs. Or trot your wares around to seaside boutiques, shops, and restaurants which sell on consignment.

If photography is your field, take pictures of other boats. Or, you can get into commercial photography by sending your photos to magazines and stock photo agencies. For help in getting started, get the annual *Photographer's Market* published by Writer's Digest Books. If you paint, try seascapes, sunsets or custom boat portraits. If you are expert in needlepoint, make finished products and custom, do-it-yourself kits. Crochet? Specialize in string bikinis. Knit? How about custom balaclavas or oiled wool sweaters? Leatherwork? Do nautical belts and wallets.

Teaching

One liveaboard I know landed in Fort Lauderdale, broke, after a sail halfway around the world. He began teaching celestial navigation. I'm frequently asked to give seminars on galley cooking or on freelance writing. A friend of mine who lived aboard for two years, started up the East Coast with a film she had made about her adventures. A superb promoter, she approached service clubs and church groups offering her program for a percentage of the gate. Often she made several hundred dollars a night, enriched the club's coffers in the bargain, and left her audience well entertained and informed. If you can teach sailing, Spanish, sailboarding, SCUBA, knitting, piloting and navigation, guitar, or anything else, you may be able to turn your talent into liveaboard funds.

If you have actual teaching credentials, you can tutor cruising kids or island families.

Freelance editing and teaching complement this boatman's liveaboard life.

Entertaining

You might put together a slide show, magic act, folksong program, or lecture that could be turned into cash as you cruise. A waterfront restaurant might want you to entertain just for tips, you could approach charter boats and offer to do your thing for their guests, or you could approach organizations as my friend did, and offer to do your program for a percentage of the gate receipts. To make a living as an entertainer you have to be very good and very lucky, but it could be just the extra few dollars a week you need to get by on your other income.

Selling Boats

Over the years we've met at least half a dozen liveaboards whose boat was also their showroom. It's a precarious living, but when you do score a sale, you score very big. The deals vary. Often you buy your boat at cost, with the understanding that you'll make it available at boat shows. During the shows, you have to endure hoards of visitors, but between shows you're free to cruise. Sometimes you're paid for appearing; sometimes you're the company's sales representative and take your share of each sale made; sometimes the deal has elements of both. A bonus for at least one of our friends who took this route was that his boat was completely equipped at wholesale, as part of his "business."

The best manufacturers for this set-up are the small, one-off boatbuilders who can't inventory a fleet of demonstrators. These are also the manufacturers, unfortunately, who have a large attrition rate. Even if you have "earned" nothing more than buying your boat-home at cost, however, this arrangement could be a bonanza for you.

Other liveaboards sell a product aboard their boat-homes, but not the boats themselves. One couple at an in-the-water boat show recently represented the manufacturer of the self-steering vane they used aboard. Others were selling houseboat charters aboard boats similar to the houseboat they lived on. If selling is your game, find a line of gear that would look good and work well aboard your boat, then offer to represent, sell, or demonstrate the line aboard your boat at in-the-water shows. The manufacturer pays your dockage and your commission and, when the show closes at night, you turn out the lights and go to bed.

Treasure Hunting

You can literally pick up money from the beach even though you're no Mel Fisher. We've had hours of fun with our metal detector, without ever trying to turn it into cash, but some of our liveaboard friends have made truly valuable finds. First, buy a fairly sophisticated detector, one that can tell the difference between a gold ring and a pull-ring from a pop can, and learn to use it. Happy hunting grounds include busy beaches on the mornings after the days of heaviest attendance. Regular beachcombers find jewelry and coins, and objects which have no resale value but for which a reward is offered. Picnic parks, and fields where there have been circus tents of fairs, are also good places to hunt. So are old dumps (your detector will find only the rusted metal but it's the old bottles that are valuable) and flats offshore from historic settlements, at low tide. Don't use a metal detector in any national park. There's a big fine. And, as a matter of good treasure-hunting manners, don't disturb archaelogical sites which could be of value to scientists someday. The hours in metal detecting can be long, and the rewards modest, but if you're beachcombing for pleasure anyway this is a way to get paid for it.

The Sciences

One winter in the Florida Keys we met some young liveaboards who spent their summers off Andros, diving for shells and other specimens for serious collectors and scientists. The profits supported them through the winter. As soon as the seas calmed and the waters warmed each spring, they left again for the islands.

The most famous liveaboard oceanographer is Jacques Cousteau, but we once met another oceanographer who lived aboard a converted air-sea rescue boat. He offered daily dive and sightseeing charters to tourists, and he promoted the operation by showing a free, professionally filmed movie each night at one of the more popular hotels. He was one of the happiest, most successful liveaboards we've met.

If you have the academic credentials to collect or scout or study or research something or other while you live aboard, remember that magic word: grant. A grant from the government or a foundation could support you while you lay the groundwork for your Nobel Prize.

Matters Medical

Here we're getting into something of a grey area because, even if you are a licensed doctor or nurse, your credentials won't be good in every state or country you visit on your boat. Still, there's a lot of fudging when you're the only medical professional for miles around. A few years back, for instance, we wrote about a Washington dentist who equipped his trawler with complete dental facilities plus liveaboard accommodations for his wife, who was also a dental technician, and their children. Each summer they cruised southeastern Alaska, ministering to people in remote logging camps. Although their primary mission was dentistry, they often ended up suturing and doing other first-aid chores which no one else could tackle.

You probably can't get into too much trouble with any authorities if

Well-known yachtsman Dick Bertram and his wife, Moppie, have been liveaboards for many years.

you take blood pressures for a couple of dollars. As a sideline you could sell the medical hardware that other liveaboards are looking for: toothache kits, inflatable splints, first-aid manuals, butterfly bandages, one of the new blood pressure devices, and other do-it-yourself medical gewgaws which cruising sailors need.

Boat Remodeling

Back in the days when we were still dreaming of living aboard, I read a book by a young couple who had made their first million before the age of thirty, by remodeling houses. They bought a rundown but basically sound house with a small down payment and moved in. They worked during the day, and spent their evenings and weekends remodeling the house. In time, they sold this house at a smart profit, invested in another sound but rundown house and used the profits to live on while they remodeled this one at a far faster clip. Soon their profits parlayed to the point where they no longer had to live among the mess of remodeling, but worked on one house while living in another.

I know one couple who have made their living for years by buying boats which are sound but cosmetically wanting, fixing them up, and selling them. As I write this they're out cruising aboard their latest boat, living on the profits from their last sale.

It is grueling, dirty work and it's far worse when you have to live aboard a boat that is constantly being sanded or varnished or torn apart. It requires a substantial grubstake, it is very costly to buy the needed lumber, paint, and fittings, and you may not be able to sell the boat after you've put all that work into it. Yet some people have exactly the knack and the drive needed to make a shopworn, sow's ear of a boat into a silk purse that sells at substantial profit. In the meantime, the boat is your home and remains so until the day you sell.

Chapter 17

Tools for the Liveaboard

~~~~~~

B efore we moved aboard *Sans Souci* we had a basement workshop
that included a drill press, radial arm saw, a workbench as long as
a royal banquet table, and endless hand and power tools, material
scraps, nuts and bolts, greases and goo's, paints and solvents, and
plenty of work and storage space. Sorting and selling all this was like
the agony of a peasant farmer selling next year's seed. We were em-
barking on a life where we could depend only on our own tools and
resourcefulness, while giving up many of the tools that Gordon had
acquired over a lifetime. Yet there was simply no other choice.

Periodically, boating magazines publish lists of tools needed by the
boat owner, but instead of giving you a pat, canned list of things *we*
think you need, Gordon and I decided to put much of the burden on
you, the liveaboard, to make your own lists. Unlike the weekend
boater, now you have to live with whatever goes wrong until you can
repair it or get it repaired. And those repairs usually have to take place
in the boat's cramped, airless, behind-the-scenes bilges and bellies,
sometimes while the boat is tossing at sea or in dockside wake, and
probably using rudimentary tools.

The weekend boater can throw in the towel, go home for a hot bath,
and get psyched up for a go-round with a broken head. The liveaboard,
however, has to deal with everything from pesty plumbing ills, to
major hull damage, to life-threatening mechanical failures—here and
now and with whatever tools and materials are available.

There are so many variables, it's hard to know where to begin your
list of needed tools. The first is your own abilities. If you don't know

which end of a screwdriver to plug into the wall socket, there's no point in carrying a tool kit worthy of a pit crew chief at Indy. On the other hand, there are probably some fittings on your boat that are in unusual sizes. Your hired mechanic or boatwright may not have tools to fit them. The same goes for spare parts. Even if you have to hire someone to install them, you should have them on hand. The more remote your roaming, the more crucial it is to have plenty of tools and spares, whether or not you know what to do with them.

At the other end of the scale is the liveaboard who will cruise far and wide and who can repair anything that can possibly go wrong with the boat. This person already knows what is needed.

Probably most of us are somewhere between. You know wood and engines, but need help with radio repairs. Or you're ace with the varnish brush and spokeshave, but wouldn't know how to grind a valve. Or you're a sailmaker *par excellence* but can't fathom marine refrigeration.

Even if you can fix everything, some tools just can't be carried except aboard the largest boats. Heaven knows, a radial arm saw would have been handy while Gordon was designing and building our self-steering vane but he had to make do with hand tools. A big vice is the workshop's workhorse, but we didn't have room for any but a pint-size one. A complete radio repair shop requires extensive test equipment; freezer repairs call for gauges and gases that you may prefer to go without.

Another variable is the type and size of your boat. You'll need one set of tools for a wood boat, one for fiberglass, others for steel or aluminum. How much elective work is ahead? Is the boat complete now or will you do some modifications while you're living aboard? Our friend Pete moved aboard his beamy motorboat while the saloon was still decorated in raw plywood and centered by a beefy band saw. Work went on while he got a head start on the joys of living aboard.

What Do You Need?

Basically, a tool is a device that will provide or increase grip, multiply effort, or cut or bore. First, sit down with every systems manual that came with the boat and all her accessories, and list the manufacturer-recommend tools and spares for maintenance and repairs. Most diesel engines, for instance, require a special tool to remove the injectors; most outboards require a puller of some sort to remove the flywheel without damage; your stuffing box nut will look and last better if you have the right-size wrenches to unlock and adjust it. The old-style, smooth-face monkey wrench is still one of the best tools for the job.

Second, go around the boat yourself listing the types and sizes of basic tools needed: screwdrivers (slot, Phillips, new high-torque types), wrenches (metric or inch), circle clip pliers for winches. Even though you don't have every size nut on your boat, it's still best to get a complete set of combination open end/box wrenches starting with about 1/4″ and up through at least 3/4″ and preferably 1″. While you don't want to get carried away with neat rows of complete sets of everything, you may encounter fittings you didn't know you had, add more later, or come to the aid of a brother boater someday.

Third, and this is the tough one, try to think through the maintenance and repair jobs you'll be making as you live aboard:

Carpentry: mast, boom, wood trim, hull, tiller, drawers, doors, hatches, coaming, bunks, galley.

Plumbing: head, water system, all pumps, tanks, fillers, filters, valves, pipes and lines, thru-hulls.

Electrical: starters, alternators, ignition, pumps, radios, lights.

Rigging: running rigging, standing rigging, sails, lines, canvas.

Mechanical: engine, transmission and shaft, AC generator, propeller, refrigeration, winches, steering, pumps.

Last, after you've made lists of the tools you'll need for all the above caretaking and repairs, make sure you also have ammunition for them all: pop rivets, crimp connectors, bits, plenty of extra saw blades, screws, nuts, bolts, nails, staples, sandpaper (aluminum oxide 120 and 220 will do almost everything you'll ever need). Two essentials are Texaco Compound L which is the best rustproofer we've found, plenty of moisture dispersant spray such as CRC 6-66, and Lubriplate 630 AA, which has proved to be our best all-purpose, waterproof grease.

All this listmaking is tedious and dull, but nobody can do it for you. Recently we went through a boating magazine article written by a renowned sailor and how-to writer who attempted to list, tool by tool, what everyone should have. His list, amazingly, was almost exactly the tools we took when we first moved aboard. Some of them proved useless; other tools we used almost daily were not on his list. Nobody else knows what you'll need in your lifestyle, on your boat, with your ability.

One more list might be made, if you have a special skill and plan to use it to make a living aboard. The tools of our trade are camera and typewriter and space had to be made for them. If you're a skilled sailmaker you may want to carry a hand-crank, heavy-duty sewing machine to ply your trade as you go. We know one liveaboard who has supported himself for years with his sewing machine. If you know radios or refrigeration or welding, diesel mechanics or caulking, carry as many of the best tools possible.

How to Buy Tools

The trouble with tools is that they are heavy, awkward, and bulky, and most of them rust. You've already cut down on the weight and bulk by making lists of things you need—rather than gathering up everything from the garage or basement that has ever turned a nut or hit a nailhead. Now shop for:

Quality

Most gripping-type tools will do the job even if they are not the most expensive ones in the store. Cutting tools, on the other hand, have wearing edges which take repeated honings. Cheap saw blades and cheap chisels are a bad buy.

Guarantee

While a guarantee might not be any good to you if you're on an uninhabited island when the tool breaks, it can be some measure of a tool's worth. Sears Craftsman line, for instance, is a time-proven classic with a lifetime guarantee, and there are Sears stores throughout North America. We have our own brand-name favorites; talk to professional mechanics about theirs.

Versatility

Some tools will do only one, infrequent task and you must have them anyway. But others will do more than one job and become the backbone of the toolbox. A hacksaw, for example, will cut almost anything from wood to metal. A wood saw will cut only wood and plastic. So if you can have only one saw, make it a hacksaw. Channel Lock pliers fill the role of pliers, pipe wrench and, in some applications, crescent wrench. A couple of good files can cut almost anything from stainless steel to wood.

Maintainability

Bare cast iron rusts quickly; forged steel plated with chrome or cadmium will last better. Tools which have working parts, such as a ratchet wrench, should come apart easily, using tools you have, for cleaning and greasing.

Independence from Shore Power

Power tools are such great servants that, even though we cruised for months at a time without access to 110-volt power, we carried a ⅜" variable speed drill, electric saber saw, and an electric soldering iron. We also, however, carried an eggbeater drill, brace and bit, stove-heated soldering iron, and keyhole saw. To depend solely on an electrical tool which could fail, and which in turn depends on dockside power or a generator or an inverter which could fail, could jeopardize a repair job that is needed quickly. There are also rechargeable power tools on the market, but they are only of interest if you have access to shore power often because they need frequent recharging. Even if you want a full arsenal of power tools for major refits, manual back-ups are still your best, get-home defense.

Caring for Tools

The first requisite is to keep salt water away from tools, but sometimes that's a tall order. If they do get salty, and have moving parts (such as pliers), give them a fresh water rinse if possible to float salt out of the joints. Others can be wiped dry. Keep salt air out of your tool boxes, which is best done with one of the spray-on moisture dispersants (WD-40, LPS, CRC 6-66). Spritz the tools any time you're going to put them away for more than a day or two. It's also good practice to put tools away sharp, ready for use the next time.

For any expensive item such as a saw, wood plane, or good chisels which are put away for weeks between uses, rub lightly with Texaco Compound L, then wrap in paper or plastic to keep the Compound L from smearing on other things. (It's messy.) If the blade is coated before you put it in the wood plane, it's doubly protected. Tools which can be dismantled, such as the threads of a pipe wrench, can be preserved for long periods with Compound L.

Keep tools in the driest place possible. We prefer a tightly sealed wood tool box because it is insulated, where plastic and metal boxes let the tools sweat.

Carrying Tools

It's nice to have variety of tool carriers because sometimes you want to take a few tools up the mast or into the chain locker for some electrical work and other times you want to load the dinghy with tools for a major hull repair. Pocketed tool "rolls" hold sets of screwdrivers and wrenches. One small toolbox can be used for the first-line-of-defense basics you grab for at the first sign of almost any breakdown. A belt carrier is good for times when you want both hands free, and some sailors are never without a belt-sheathed bosun's knife. A plastic bucket is an ideal carrier for bulky, unrelated items. So is an inexpensive, household cleaner caddy found in discount stores. Both have handles and can be carried easily with one hand. A plastic milk carrier makes a big, two-hand load for major, move-around jobs. Such carriers also make good dividers for large stowage areas, because you can fill them with smaller jars of screws, cans of paint, or other hard-to-corral items.

Books and Manuals

The most important tools aboard your boat may not be in the toolbox. They are the how-to manuals written by manufacturers specifically for the equipment on your boat. Take pains to preserve these documents because sometimes even the best mechanic can't guess at the torque settings for your engine or know that certain types of lubes are wrong for your winches.

Shop marine bookstores and catalogues for how-to books which will supplement your own skills in engines, joinerwork, wiring, canvas work, or whatever. Two sources of discount books are BOAT/US, 880 S. Pickett St., Alexandria, VA 22304, and Dolphin Book Club, 485 Lexington Ave., New York, NY 10017. Both require membership.

Chapter 18

Cleaning and Pests

E ven housecleaning has changed dramatically in the past few years with the advent of new cleaning products and fiberglass fixtures, but keeping "house" aboard a boat-home is different still because you're dealing with materials you've never had to clean before. Plumbing may be delicate plastics which can't take harsh chemicals. Besides, you don't want to put them into your holding tank or, worse still, your lake or the ocean. Salt crystals build up in the head. Your overheads are made of a spongy, sound-dampening vinyl or rough fiberglass. Your "walls" are varnished or carpeted. Your carpets fill with crumbs and sand and salt. You wres ᴇ with how best to clean acrylics and plastics and gel coats and marine paints.

The primary cleaning rule in any situation is to start with the mildest product possible, then get gradually tougher as needed. Mild soap and water, followed by a good rinse, are your best cleaning agents. Conversely, kitchen cleaners and other abrasive/acid type powders can etch, erode, and create a rough surface that is ideal for farming mildew or absorbing new stains.

I found that a mild ammonia water solution was best for restoring the shine to our varnished bulkheads, which dulled regularly from all the cooking projects in our small boat. I tried all types of furniture polishes, from old-type oils to the new cleaner-sprays, but none worked as well as the ammonia water.

The new acrylic ports, hatches and windshields are harder than earlier plastics but they are still susceptible to scratches from grit—and that includes any particles in the rag you're using to clean them. Use

199

lots and lots of water (even if you have to use salt water at first to loosen dried-on salt crystals) to float away grime. Add a little vinegar for shine, but keep ammonia, abrasive cleaners, some commercial window-cleaning products (read the labels), paper towels, and waxes away from acrylics. If your plastic windows become so scratched that they are distracting when you're looking out, look for mildly abrasive polishes which are sold especially for plastic windows. If your marina doesn't carry one, try the fixed base operator at the nearest airport. For really bad scratches you may need jeweler's rouge, and the advice of a professional glazier. For glass ports, vinegar or ammonia water are cheap and effective cleaners, and crumpled newspaper makes a good scrubber-shiner.

Vinegar and fresh water worked best on the salt build-up in the head, and I used a vegetable brush as a toilet brush because it was the right shape but took up less room.

For cleaning and protecting the porcelain stove, fans, and almost any other metal aboard, we used Johnson's J-Wax. Special new cleaning products have been formulated for the new epoxy paints, plastic fabrics, and synthetic floor and wall coverings. Since these actually feed and restore the surface, as well as clean, it's best to get specific products recommended by manufacturers.

There are new commercial cleaners on the market for fiberglass galley and head fixtures. Don't ever touch yours with an abrasive cleanser or it's the beginning of the end. Small scratches dull the shine, the gel coat absorbs more dirt, and more scrubbing with harsher cleaners is needed as time goes on. The same goes for plastic seat covers, which will mop up in minutes with one of the favorite sink cleansers. After a few cleanings you'll notice that the gloss is gone and it's downhill from there.

When everything else fails, use bleaching, gritty kitchen cleaners. More effective still, we find, is a cleanser called Zud for otherwise-intractable dock rash and waterline mustache on past-their-prime fenders and topsides. But use such cleansers only as a last resort, and use them conservatively.

Mildew is most liveaboards' most vexsome enemy but you may be surprised to hear that we had far more problems with it in Vermont and Martha's Vineyard than in steamy Florida. The most important preventive is ventilation and cleanliness. When you get up in the morning and the boat is damp below, and under awnings and dodgers from condensation, wipe down the worst of it and get the breeze blowing through to dry everything.

Rotate all stored clothing, linens, and other fabrics. If items aren't worn for several months, wash them anyway. Make sure everything is completely clean and dry before it's stowed—and that goes double for foul weather gear, which is best stowed in a separate locker and never with other clothing. Turn the mattress each time you change the bed; air everything in the sunshine as often as possible. Don't, however, spread mattresses and pillows on a salty deck or they'll drag salt crystals below, the salt will draw moisture out of the night air, and the mattress will be forever damp.

When you're repainting, mix an anti-fungal agent (available at marine paint stores) into the paint. We use one called Inter-Tox made by International Paint Co., and it kept each new coat of paint from mildewing for several years. When you're cleaning, avoid using any more detergent or bleach than is absolutely necessary, and rinse repeatedly. I believe their residue feeds mildew because it always seemed to grow faster after a good soaping.

When mildew really gets a good start, a strong broth of detergent, bleach and vinegar is the best cleaner. Never, by the way, mix bleach with ammonia because toxic fumes are generated. Scrub gently with a brush, then rinse well. I've never found anything that will get mildew out of fabric better than bleach which will also, unfortunately, fade any color but white. As a last, desperate measure, you might try color removers which are sold in the dye departments of grocery and variety stores.

For tiles, grout, shower stalls and curtains, vinyl canopies, boat tops, and painted surfaces there is a special product sold in grocery stores and called instant mildew remover. It is sprayed on, and it fades the stain instantly but be sure to read the precautions on the label. It's basically a strong bleaching agent.

If you're lucky enough to have a shower aboard, you're unlucky enough to have special cleaning problems. Soap scum and scale build up, more dampness is brought into the boat with the steamy water, the teak grate gets gummy, and all sorts of agricultural unpleasantries start growing in your shower sump or bilge. Conventional cleaning products, used more often than you ever thought possible, are the answer. Keep the teak clean and well treated with your favorite teak product. Just don't put oil over soap scum. If the sump's fungal crop can't be controlled any other way, ask air conditioner service people about a fungicide they use to control growths in condensate.

Ann Bolderson, who is one of the best boatkeepers I've ever met, told me her secret for the crystal-clear shower curtains aboard the Bolderson's charter boat. At the same time you're laundering the bath towels, add a cup of ammonia to the soapy, warm water (don't add bleach) and then put the shower curtain into the washer. Let it go through the wash cycle, and the tumbling towels will scrub away the stains, mildew, and water spots from the plastic. Then stop the machine before it drains and spins (usually in a laundromat the machine stops when you open the lid), pull out the shower curtain, and immediately wipe it down with a sponge. Let the towels complete the cycle.

There's a limit to what can be done with a whisk broom and dustpan, and I do recommend having a small 12-volt or 110-volt vacuum cleaner aboard. It's the only way to get crumbs and dust out of all the corners and crevices a boat has. In port, I used a throw rug in the galley area where so much debris accumulated. This could be shaken outdoors several times a day, and saved a lot of sweeping. Another preventive is a good door mat on the dock and another at the companionway even if you, as we did, take off shoes before going below. There are lots of new ones which do a good scraping job and allow particles to fall through to the dock below. At the companionway we used a softer, more absorbent mat. Underway, of course, all mats were stowed because they don't provide firm footing.

Good screens keep out flying insects, and I recommend that everything be screened—including ventilators, dorade boxes, and even the smallest opening where a mosquito could squeeze through. If you'll be boating in coastal or island areas where sand flies are a problem (we've battled them from Nova Scotia to the Bahamas), screens alone won't keep them out but a smearing of kerosene helps. Better still is a product called Screen Pruf which is a toxic, oily substance to be put on screens. It's sold commonly in Florida and perhaps you can find it in your area too.

The only insects that have ever given us much trouble have been roaches, although spiders too are persistent pests when you don't keep on the move. I've known some liveaboards who were never without ants aboard, too. When we were at dock for more than a night at a time, I sprayed the docklines weekly or after each rain. Although Florida roaches can fly fair distances and get aboard anyway, this did cut down on the ant and spider invasions. I also used one of the residual-action, commercial ant sprays around the cockpit and companionway and, when ants became a real problem, set out a wet sponge which had been dipped in a mixture of sugar and boric acid. Ants found it irresistible and soon disappeared.

In ten years we had only one roach infestation (if you ever see more than one, that's an infestation because there are dozens unseen for every one you see.) The easiest way to check for roaches, even if you never see one in the daytime, is to get up at night and snap on the light. If you have roaches, they'll probably be disporting all over the galley.

Roach cures start with prevention. Don't bring them aboard. They are most common in the corrugations of cardboard boxes, but I've found egg clusters on can labels, and roaches in potato sacks and egg cartons. The eggs, by the way, look like a dark, syrup blob about the size of a teardrop. If roaches have been invading food packages, the hole is a small oval that is probably not more than ⅛" long.

If your boat has a wet bilge, a few drops of chlordane or another poison recommended by a good gardening store will do the job. The more complicated your boat, the harder it will be to rout roaches because they can last forever behind ceilings and deep in bilges. Our boat was dry and simple, so when I saw two roaches at once one night, we started dismantling things. Egg clusters were found everywhere,

A night-time stowaway, this raccoon lived aboard uninvited for several days.

indicating that a much larger invasion had been planned by our original colonists.

Everything was scrubbed and sprayed with one of the commercial roach products. Then, while the boat was torn limb from timber, I sprinkled 20 Mule Team Borax everywhere. Boric acid is the ingredient in most roach remedies, and I've also mixed it heavily with sugar as a roach trap. I haven't, however, had much luck with roach tablets and traps. The most effective poison seemed to be the widespread sprinkling of the borax, which the roaches couldn't avoid in their movement. They lick themselves clean, ingest the borax, and it's curtains.

When we had our house built, I sprinkled this same product under areas where sinks and cabinets would be installed, and we've never had a roach problem. If you're building a boat, it costs very little in time and money to dose any enclosed areas with borax (provided it's compatible with the building material) before you seal them.

I have heard of boats so badly invaded by roaches that the only solution was to have them tented and fumigated, but the alert and ready liveaboard should be able to get control long before this point is reached.

We've been visited by rats many times during our liveaboard nights, and it was always comforting to know that every vent or opening into the boat was firmly covered with brass screening. Rats and docks go together like bagels and lox, so expect them and be closed up against them. No matter how warm the night, we never sleep at a dock with hatches open. Indeed, a boat should be able to ventilate well with the hatches closed because you have to close hatches at sea even on the hottest days.

Of the many liveaboards I've known who had serious rat problems, most had cats or dogs so you can't count on them as a defense. One couple got a rat aboard while they were rafted, third boat from the dock! Rat guards, the cone-shaped metal barriers used by large ships, aren't much help on a yacht which is next to the dock and low enough for the rat to hop aboard. So carry a trap, close up at night, and don't neglect the screening.

Chapter 19

Safety and Security
When a Boat Is Your Home

~~~~~~

T he law tells you many of the safety items your boat must have: fire
extinguishers, day and night flares, and life jackets. In addition,
the type and scope of your boating will suggest additional purchases—a
life raft, safety harnesses, solar still, Emergency Position Indicator
Radio Beacon (EPIRB) and so on if you'll do extensive offshore boating. One good guide to such equipping is *Sea Sense* (International
Marine Publishing) by Richard Henderson. *Piloting, Seamanship and
Small Boathandling* (Hearst Marine Books) is also a complete guide to
safety equipment. *The National Fisherman*, a monthly tabloid published by International Marine in Camden, Maine, goes primarily to
commerical fishermen but it's a good source of information on safety
gear needed in the open sea by sailors who venture out in all weather.

However, there are problems special to all liveaboards. Your common sense dictates more than the bare, legal minimum. This boat is,
after all, your home. The possessions you have aboard are not just
vacation frills but they include priceless family heirlooms such as
paintings or the sterling flatware, a cache of jewelry or collector coins,
firearms, a television or two, perhaps expensive electronics such as
video games, a stereo, a video cassette recorder—not even counting
the boat's radios and electronics.

You need to protect your possessions from theft and fire. Most
important of all, you and your family prepare and eat every meal
aboard, and you sleep aboard every night. It's important that you have
protection night and day, when you're aboard and when you're away.

Thanks to an explosion in smart new electronics, and sophisticated new anti-theft devices in recent years, there are many ways to protect your loved ones and your possessions but before we get into them, there is a far more basic need and that is to know how to make use of what you already have. A British cruising sailor we met in Key West told us he had nearly drowned a few days before, in shallow water and in sight of his boat—all because his cruising companion didn't know where he kept the extra coils of rope.

Our cruising friend was exploring a shoal in the dinghy and lost an oar just as the wind freshened. He was out of sight of land, and when the tide changed, he started drifting out to sea. The water was only waist deep so he began walking the dink back to the boat. Then as the water got deeper, he began swimming, pushing the dinghy ahead of him. As the skies got darker and the wind stronger, his strength began to wane. He might have sacrificed the dinghy, and made a dash for the boat, but he needed the dinghy's flotation now. The crewman said later that he'd thought of a number of ways to help, such as floating a long rope out to the dinghy. But he had no idea where the ropes were kept,

On this boat, bars across portholes keep the ship's cat from escaping in port, and also slow down burglars. Keep your valuables away from unprotected windows.

nor how to operate the old-fashioned, British-made radio to call for help.

This story has a happy ending because our friend did make it back to the boat, with the dinghy, before his strength was gone. "I can't get over the irony of it all," he shook his head as he told the story. "All through it I kept thinking that I'd survived crossing the entire, bloody Atlantic and now I was going to die in shoulder-deep water."

But not every such story ends well, even though the boats themselves have every safety device in the world. In one case, radio eavesdroppers listened in horror as a woman screamed for help after her husband fell overboard in the Gulf Stream. She did not know how to bring the boat about and it sailed on, steered by an autopilot, while her husband disappeared in the wake. His body was never found. In others, we've listened helplessly for hours while Coast Guard rescuers tried to get a fix on a skipper in trouble who was unable to tell them where he was.

Everyone aboard your boat should know what emergency equipment is available, where it is, and how to use it. Even young family

All boats, large and small, liveaboard and otherwise, must have flares aboard to signal for help.

Every adult aboard should know where emergency equipment is kept and, if possible, how to operate it. Responsible children should know where to find emergency gear.

members can learn how to throw a flotation device overboard, how to signal S.O.S. with a flashlight, how to operate a fire extinguisher, and other lifesaving skills.

Your extinguishers have to be recharged yearly, to satisfy both the Coast Guard and your insurance company. Instead of merely leaving the extinguishers at the re-charge station, take the family with you and ask to set off the charges yourselves. (It's best not to shoot them off anywhere else, because some extinguisher contents are highly corrosive. Re-charge stations have a special place for disposing of the old charge.) This gives every family member a real feel for how hard it is to push or pull the levers and rings, how far the charge shoots, and how long the stream lasts.

Everyone in the family should know where every piece of emergency gear is stowed, and, if not how to use it, then how to get it out of the locker or out of its clip to pass it to a responsible person. As soon as they are old enough, children should know how to don their own life jackets—in the dark and in the water as well as under calm, dry, safe circumstances—and know who is in charge of younger children who can't fend for themselves.

Hands-on experience with safety gear is so important that Wayne Williams, a retired Air Force safety expert, gives a one-day water survival course which is open to anyone whose hobbies or profession takes them on, over, or near the water. Children as young as eight have taken this no-nonsense course and have learned to set off day and night flares by feel alone, to get into life jackets, to climb into life boats, and even how to use a signal mirror. After a half day of lectures and slides, students actually get into the water for hands-on experience with solar stills, the various collars and seats that are used by rescue professionals to lift people out of the water, and other lifesaving gear.

Williams' fund of anecdotes is based on his years of working with survivors and of investigating accidents. He tells of one group who nearly died at sea because they couldn't inflate a liferaft. They didn't realize how hard a tug on the lanyard was required. Another went thirsty for hours—not knowing that the raft's emergency kit had gone overboard but was still there, held by a safety line. "We've taken experienced airplane passengers who have seen life jacket demon-

Specially designed life jackets suit the special needs of infants and children.

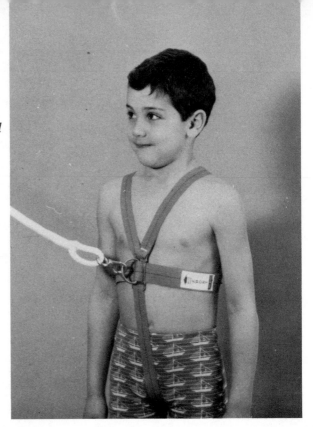

Life harnesses in small sizes are also available.

strations a hundred times, and most of them couldn't put their jackets on properly—even though we were standing on terra firma, without rush or panic," Williams says as he hammers at the importance of firsthand experience with lifesaving gear.

There are other water safety courses available throughout the country, most of them designed for professional seamen, pilots, and oil rig workers. Williams' course is especially recommended because it is affordable, expertly taught, and includes in-the-water drills using real equipment. For details, write Wayne Williams, Nova University Institute for Survival Technology, 3301 College Ave., Ft. Lauderdale, FL 33314.

While man-overboard and life jacket drills can be done anywhere, and fire extinguisher practice is a good idea at re-charge time, inflating your life raft unnecessarily is something else again. Check your instruction manual. Inflation on land, without the cushioning and warming effects of water, could injure the fabric of your raft. It's important to the reliability and long life of your raft that it be inflated, checked, and repacked by experts.

In addition to learning about emergency gear, some things should be learned by all liveaboard families, even those who never leave the dock:

1. Everyone aboard should know how to open hatches from the inside. There are dozens of different hatch designs, most of them difficult, and many of them too heavy or tight for children. Have an alternate plan of help or escape in such cases.

2. Adults and responsible children should know where the boat is. While this may sound absurd, think of how you'd explain to the fire department, police, or rescue squad how to find your boat by road. If your area has a fire boat, could you explain how to find your boat from the water? Do you know where there's a telephone? What coin is needed? Where to find one? Underway, keep a running check on the boat's position and make sure more than one person aboard knows it. Most experienced, seagoing families take this for granted, but we once monitored a long radio exchange while we were on a crowded Tennesse lake. A heart attack victim was taken ashore and someone was giving him CPR, but no one could figure out how to tell the ambulance to reach the victim by road.

3. Adults and responsible children should know how to operate the radio, find the emergency channels, and give necessary information.

4. Kids, as well as adults, should know where to find a flashlight or a Cyalume light stick if emergency light is needed.

5. Learn how to recognize a collision course. One way that can be easily understood by anyone aboard is that when another vessel stays at the same relative point on your boat and continues to grow larger while you maintain a constant heading, you're going to meet. At night when it's difficult to see and translate navigation lights, this technique is very helpful in giving early warning.

6. Any time fuels are being used aboard your boat (heating, cooking, engine, generator) be alert for any signs of carbon monoxide poisoning. Symptoms include headache, ringing in the ears, and perhaps a cherry red appearance to the skin. Children are the most vulnerable. A cluster of houseboats, anchored in a quiet lake under the shadow of protective hills, ran their generators all night so the families could have air conditioning. Fumes hung low over the water on the breezeless

night. Fortunately, when a child got up in the night and complained of headache and nausea, one of the adults recognized the mark of carbon monoxide—an odorless killer. Sometimes, in a boat underway, people down below can be suffering from carbon monoxide poisoning while those on deck, unaffected, push on.

7. No matter how landlocked your boat, have an occasional man-overboard drill. Obviously this is a greater worry when you're at sea in heavy weather, but there are a surprising number of overboard accidents at the dock, in flat calm. The usual reason: a male, sometimes after too much to drink, goes to the rail to urinate and falls in. Throw in an added element such as swift current, very cold water, restrictive clothing, a mild heart attack or stroke, or an injury during the fall, and tragedy results. All liveaboards, even those who never leave the dock, should know what will be thrown overboard to help someone in distress in the water, and should keep that equipment handy and in good repair, and should have some plan for getting a victim back aboard or to the nearest shore.

8. Boating families who keep on the go are familiar with the drill of getting underway, but for those who are comfortably dockbound it's good to have an occasional practice "scramble." If another boat on the pier catches fire, you want to get yours out—safely but quickly, before the fire spreads. Know how to get moving, and where the boat will be taken. Discuss just who is authorized to make such a move. Everybody aboard? The eldest child? Only certain children or crew?

We've had two such emergencies. Once we were eating a leisurely breakfast when we looked out to see that our direction had changed. We were riding to a borrowed mooring and the line parted, leaving us adrift in a tiny, crowded harbor.

Automatically, we were able to get underway while remembering to run the engine blower and haul in the frayed mooring line before it could wrap around the propellor. Another time, we were ashore enjoying an outdoor movie, when fire broke out on a houseboat on the dock. Our boat was not in danger that time, but other boats couldn't be moved in time and were damaged. Some liveaboards who spend a lot of time at docks actually keep hatchets where they can reach them readily, to chop docklines if an immediate escape is called for.

9. If you live in a marina, take a cue from the Neighborhood Watch movement and organize against crime. Since so many boats don't have telephones aboard, you'll need a plan of action for what to do once something suspicious is spotted.

10. Teach everyone aboard how to pull a master switch, shore power plug, or circuit breaker to turn off shore power in an emergency. Even people experienced in using appliances and power tools sometimes drop their guard and get zapped by the combination of electricity, improper grounds, and water. Gordon once glanced up from his work to see that the skipper of the boat docked ahead of us was standing there, an odd look on his face, frozen to his power sander. He jumped to the dock and yanked the right plug, and our neighbor sagged to the dock. Fortunately he was all right. In other cases, CPR and other emergency measures are needed later, so, if you know first aid as well as how to turn off the juice, so much the better.

Security

Anti-theft devices have come a long way since Joshua Slocum sprinkled carpet tacks on his decks to stifle stealthy night-boarding thieves. There are countless snares to choose from, some designed for use in homes and others engineered for boat use.

Basically, such devices break down into a couple of categories, beginning with locks. In addition to the obvious ways to lock your boat, you'll find special locks for gas and water caps, outboards, boat trailers, boat trailers' spare tires, trailer hitches, individual electronics, and other special needs. You'll find them in boating catalogues and marinas.

The choice of alarms is so vast it can be confusing, but basically the liveaboard is concerned with two things in addition to the reliability and effectiveness which any alarm should have: seaworthiness, that is, resistance to dampness and corrosion, as well as ability to discern between normal boat motion and boarders, and independent power supply. Many of the burglar alarms sold for home use depend on household power. It's too easy for a burglar to unplug your shore power cord, so any alarm on your boat should have back-up battery power. Even if it's a 12-volt device that runs off ships' batteries, you'll have extra insurance if the alarm has an alternate choice of power if the main battery fails. Other household alarms read heat or motion, such as an intruder crossing a room however silently. Such alarms have problems on boats because they can be triggered by natural motion or curtains moving as the boat rocks in a wake.

The On Watch is one alarm engineered especially for boats. It has its own power supply, which is good for 6-9 months before recharging. You can hook up its sensors to alert you if shore power stops, if any hatches are entered, or if a pressure-sensitive mat is stepped on, or it can be activated by certain sounds. You can set the alarm to activate a strobe light or siren, instantly or after a delay of up to one minute if you prefer. You can also have it shout "Burglar! Burglar!" or "Fire! Fire!" if you like. This combination of audible and visible alarms is a nice feature in a crowded marina because, should a break-in occur when you're not home, it could take authorities precious minutes to discover from which boat a bell or siren is coming. You can even get a long-distance paging system that will alert you up to eight miles away, by pocket pager, if your boat is being boarded while you're shopping or beachcombing ashore. For full information, write Cord Marine Industries, 8800 N. Bayshore Drive, Miami, FL 33138.

Another multi-purpose alarm is made by Safeguard Systems. The compact 12-volt device can report to you on forced entries, refrigerator failure, rising bilge water, and fumes. It's made by Wolsk Safeguard Systems, P.O. Box 11741, Lexington, KY 40511. The entire control box can be held in the palm of your hand.

One catalogue house that specializes in security equipment is Mountain West, P.O. Box 10780, Phoenix, AZ 85064. They carry all types of readymade alarms, components for making custom systems, how-to books, and such aids as engraving tools for marking your possessions. Locally, hardware stores and electronics stores such as Radio Shack are also a good source of basic components for designing your own burglar alarm system.

Other Alarms

Two very simple, inexpensive, battery-operated alarms are offered by Datasonic, 255 E. Second St., Mineola, NY 11501. One is the Flood Alert, which sounds when it becomes so much as damp. The

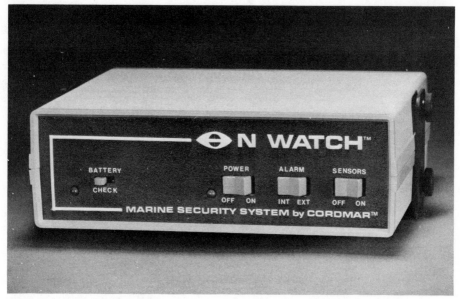

Cordmar's On Watch Security System can alert you to fire and theft with lights, a voice shouting Burglar or Fire, or alarms of your choice.

This Safeguard alarm is tiny but can monitor fumes, bilge water, break-in, and various temperatures. It can also report on battery status.

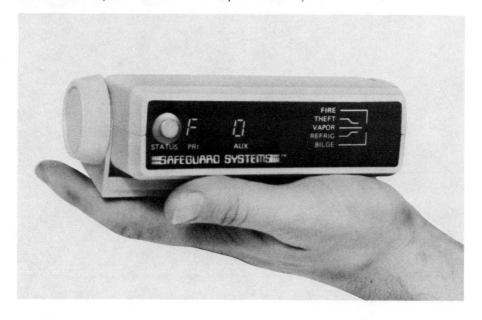

Shop carefully for the smart new electronics to find out what they can and cannot do for you.

A fuel solenoid shut-off switch is a safety feature, allowing instant gasoline turn-off in case of trouble. If hidden, it can also prevent thieves from starting up the engine.

other is Freez-Alert which sounds if your freezer warms up above 25-28 degrees.

In addition to the many companies which make burglar alarms of various types, there are alerts and alarms for almost anything that can go wrong aboard your boat, and new devices are coming on the market all the time. There are, for example, countless sniffers to detect fumes, an alert that lets you know if your bilge pump has been running more than it should, fire alarms, alarms that go off if your raw water cooling flow is interrupted, off-course alarms, and even alarms that detect radar. To keep up with developments, read marine catalogues, go to boat shows, and get one of the yearly equipment guides such as those published by *Sail* and *Yachting* magazines.

Guns

Whether or not to carry guns aboard your floating home is a topic that is usually discussed with too much heat and too little light. If you have guns in your home, you'll probably want them in your boat-home. If you're against guns, moving aboard will not make guns look more attractive to you.

The one thing that should be pointed out about guns on boats is that they complicate things when you cruise from state to state or among various foreign countries and you have to keep conforming to diverse, sometimes punitive, gun laws. So if you carry guns aboard, be prepared for some extra paperwork and delay. If you feel that guns should be a part of your safety set-up, one guide is *Tappan on Survival* which is available from Janus Press, P.O. Box 578, Rogue River, OR 97537. The book covers food and retreats, as well as weapons.

Chapter 20

The Road Back

E very proper story has a beginning, a middle, and an end. For some people the end of the liveaboard story is tragic—the loss of a boat, the death of a spouse, the break-up of a relationship. For many others there is merely a petering out, a retreat into a dreary acceptance of a liveaboard life which has lost its drive, excitement, and sense of adventure.

Liveaboards are a strange lot, and are the first to admit it. Most of us even admit it proudly. Some of the most selfless, hard-working, caring, competent, resourceful, intelligent, and friendly people we've met have been part of the liveaboard family.

This family, however, also includes some of the most sour, arrogant, defensive, and bitter people we've encountered. Among the sourest and most defensive are those who cling to the liveaboard image even though they have secretly grown to hate the life. They've made some jut-jawed vow, it seems, and have too much pride to give up this way of life and commit to a new one.

We're happy to report that these two extremes, the tragedies and the sourpusses, are in the minority. Most of us simply came to the end of the liveaboard story and moved on to new challenges. Some people end the story in triumph. Don and Sue Moesly, for instance, set themselves a goal of circumnavigating in about five years and then going back to land life and jobs. This is what they did.

Others gradually lose interest in living aboard (although not necessarily in boating) and gavotte happily into exciting new horizons.
220 Chuck and Chris Grey are an inspiration to people who want to lick

challenge after challenge. Both had successful careers in Chicago before they went into boating. They crossed the Atlantic and sailed in the Mediterranean. They did well in the charter business in the Caribbean and the Bahamas. One of their goals was to sail southeastern Alaska. Mission accomplished.

In summer, they traveled in their trailer, started reading up on ranching, and ended up with a cattle-breeding operation in Oregon. In time they sold that and built a home on a magnificent coast in the San Juan Islands, finished another motor sailer, and started sailing their favorite haunts in the Northwest. Every Christmas we wait eagerly for word from the Greys on what new worlds they have chosen to conquer—and conquer they do.

One couple gave up living on a boat to live on a farm and raise goats. Another couple have built a saltbox house in the beautiful woods of New Hampshire. Others lived aboard long enough to get a grubstake, then parlayed a small down payment into a fortune in Florida real estate.

In his book *Yen for a Yacht* (EPM Publications), Robert Woodbury gave one of the best descriptions of how some liveaboards move along by moving off the boat. He describes "island fever" which comes on slowly and subtly. He no longer reads menus in the island restaurants because he knows them by heart. He regrets his loss of privacy while making his living by chartering his boat on a small island: he couldn't go anywhere without meeting someone he knew.

Even though we kept on the go, never staying in one spot for more than a few weeks, we sometimes felt this loss of privacy, too. At anchor, everybody knows you're at home when the dinghy is trailing astern. In a marina, you can't have lunch, or do a project in the cockpit, without an audience. We've even had a few curious clods come clammering aboard for a look-see. Imagine someone bursting into your house that way!

For us, some aspects of the liveaboard life eventually began to chafe. One was a bad experience in a boatyard. That reminded us how vulnerable we would always be as long as we had to depend on others to haul our boat/home. We were dependent in other ways, too, for land transportation, and for docks at least part of the time. Although our lives were no longer ruled by corporations, we were ruled just as strictly by wind, waves, tides, seasons, and petty officialdom both at home and abroad.

There was the gradual realization that most cocktail hour conversation with other liveaboards boiled down to a couple of topics. One was anchors. Another was how clever we all were to get out of Youngstown or Greenwich or Arlington Heights. It was often like Bob Woodbury's memorized menu. We'd heard it all and said it all before.

Gradually one becomes less excited about the options available while living aboard. The mind strays to the things which could be done with a different boat, or some land for a garden. If only the boat would go faster than six knots, or if only you had room to have a real library of both books and tapes. As long as everyone in the family/crew gets the same notions at the same time, and a transition can be accomplished with mutual caring and cooperation, leaving the liveaboard life can be as rewarding and exhilarating as moving aboard.

Some ex-liveaboards go back to old careers, some to another form of subsistance life such as farming. Most, however, stay on or near the water, and in boat-related careers: starting a dive shop, managing a hotel in the West Indies, opening a restaurant on the waterfront, selling boats, repairing boats, building boats, drawing boats, promoting boats, or advertising boats.

One fellow we know makes a specialty of painting gold leaf, and makes a living in boatyards painting name-boards. Bob and Ann Bolderson were for years the most successful charterboat professionals in the Bahamas, then took a job crewing a luxurious company boat. Ann's cooking skills are so legendary she once rated a full page in the New York *Times*; between cruises she caters dinners and cocktail parties aboard Fort Lauderdale's most glittering yachts.

The list of après-liveaboard success stories is endless.

There's a happy ending to our liveaboard story too. Just as we didn't throw a temper tantrum back in Illinois, walk off the job, and run away to sea, we didn't rush out of the boat life either. As our fortunes fared better, we saw we could afford to have a house while still keeping the boat.

Others might pool everything and buy a bigger boat, but we never saw a boat of any size that we wanted more than *Sans Souci*. A boat is still a boat, and we wanted occasionally to see mountains, forests, trout streams, and deserts. If we put all our resources into a larger boat we would have more comfort but still a limited travel range.

Living aboard can be indescribably satisfying and enriching. We don't know where we would be now if we hadn't taken that step, but it's unlikely we would be living in a pleasant little Florida town, writing books and articles, having lunch together every day, and cruising anywhere the notion takes us.

When the time comes for you to leave the liveaboard life behind, look upon it as another adventure. You *can* go home again. When and if you do, you will be infinitely richer for having chosen, for whatever length of time, a boat as your home.

Life aboard, like anywhere else, is what you make it.

PHOTO CREDITS

Jacket: Queene Hooper

A.C.R.: 209 bottom
Aladdin: 94 bottom, 95 both
Roy Attaway: 28 top and bottom, 30 top and bottom,
    39 bottom, 40, 48 both, 52 both, 147
Coleman: 94 top
Goldberg Marine: 211 both, 212
Gordon Groene: 21, 44 both, 45 both, 62 all, 63, 64 both,
    74 all, 75 all, 99 both, 101 all, 102, 103 both,
    181, 207, 218 bottom
Queene Hooper: 165 both, 174
Dan Nerney: 29 bottom, 38 bottom, 39 top, 51 top
Norcold: 72
Olin Corp.: 208, 209 top
Jeff Perkell: 11, 24, 32 top, 34 both, 43, 46 top,
    56, 77, 78 all, 80, 91, 92, 93, 104, 113, 114 both,
    127, 128 both, 134 all, 143, 168, 184, 188, 204, 223
Ray Jefferson Electronics: 218 top
Stanley Rosenfeld: 38 top, 46 bottom, 88, 191 both
Terry Walton: 167 both
Grady White: 66, 67
Wolsk Associates: 217 both